W9-BXX-185

# Tofu
## MANIA

# BRITA HOUSEZ

## Add Tofu to 120 of Your Favorite Dishes

MARLOWE & COMPANY
NEW YORK

Published by
Marlowe & Company
A Division of the Avalon Publishing Group
841 Broadway, 4th floor
New York, NY 10003

TOFU MANIA: *Add Tofu to 120 of Your Favorite Dishes*
Copyright © 1998, 2000 by Brita Housez

All rights reserved. No part of this book may be reproduced in whole or in part without written permission from the publishers, except by reviewers who may quote brief excerpts in connection with a review in a newspaper, magazine, or electronic publication; nor may any part of this book be reproduced, stored in a retrieval system, or transmitted in any form or by any means electronic, mechanical, photocopying, recording, or other, without written permission from the publisher.

Nutritional Analysis by Heather Dzioba, M.Sc. (Nutr.)

Photography by Patricia Holdsworth
Patricia Holdsworth Photography, Regina, Saskatchewan

Dishes and accessories shown on cover courtesy of the MacKenzie Art Gallery Gift Shop, Regina, Saskatchewan
Front cover photograph: Fresh Berry Clafoutis, pp.170–171.

Library of Congress Cataloging-in-Publication Data

Housez, Brita.
    Tofu mania : add tofu to 120 of your favorite dishes / by Brita Housez.
        p.  cm.
    Includes index.
    ISBN 1-56924-601-7
    1. Cookery (Tofu)    I. Title.

TX814.5.T63 H68 2000
641.6'5655—dc21

00-056216

9 8 7 6 5 4 3 2

*Designed by Pauline Neuwirth, Neuwirth & Associates, Inc.*

Distributed by Publishers Group West
Printed in the United States of America

For my mother, Ruth Stolz,
who inspired me with her love of healthy cooking.

# CONTENTS

## Breakfast, Brunch, and Lunch

## Appetizers, Dips, Spreads, and Sauces

## Soups and Salads

## Vegetables and Side Dishes

## Meatless Main Dishes

## Fish and Meat Main Dishes

# Desserts

# ACKNOWLEDGMENTS

I WOULD LIKE to thank the following people whose encouragement and assistance helped me to persevere with this project: my friend Karen Neal, whose communication skills led me to Centax; Bev Jong, whose efficient typing kept me organized; Margo Embury of Centax, whose people skills and expertise took the strain out of the publishing process.

Special thanks to my family for their overwhelming support: my daughter Bettina who tested many of the recipes; my daughter Lara and my partner, Hermann Ludwig, who enthusiastically taste-tested my recipes these past three-and-one-half years, offering me many helpful suggestions along the way.

# INTRODUCTION

TOFU *MANIA!* DID you know that it is sweeping across North America? Let me tell you why it's time you joined the craze for one of the world's least expensive, most good-for-you foods. You probably have been hearing, more and more frequently, that tofu—a cake of pressed curds made from coagulated soy milk—is good for your health. But you may also have the mistaken idea that tofu is only eaten by vegetarians, vegans, and other super-health-conscious eaters. This is just not so! Tofu is for *everyone*—and more and more of us are discovering this fact. Hear it loudly and clearly: You absolutely do not need to be a vegetarian in order to eat tofu and benefit from its many healthy qualities. I have written *Tofu Mania* for *all* health-conscious cooks who, having repeatedly heard and read about the disease-fighting properties of tofu, are eager to include tofu in their daily cooking, but who don't relish the prospect of eating tofu stir-fry every night of the week!

Although tofu has been popular in China and Japan for centuries—and available in the western world for over thirty years—its popularity in the United States has begun to skyrocket only in the last several years. The newfound enthusiasm for tofu is in part the result of recent scientific studies—studies that are repeatedly concluding that tofu, along with other soy foods, can treat or prevent diseases such as breast, uterine, endometrial, ovarian, colon and prostate cancers, heart disease and strokes, osteoporosis and kidney disease, as well as relieve menopausal symptoms such as night sweats and hot flashes. Moreover, bone density and bone mineral content have been shown to increase significantly with high soy diets. According to scientific research, soy's beneficial effects on health are due to phyto-chemicals which occur naturally in plants. These biologically active sub-stances contain compounds called isoflavones, genistein and daidzein, that are similar to the natural estrogen produced in humans. It is these com-pounds which are largely responsible for the numerous health benefits provided by soy foods.

In addition to protecting us from life-threatening diseases, tofu is high in protein yet low in calories: 3 ounces (100 g) of medium tofu has only 75 calories, while 3 ounces (100 g) of firm tofu has only 145 calories. Low-fat tofu is now available in many supermarkets, further reducing the calorie count. Tofu is also free of cholesterol and lactose, low in fats and rich in vitamins, iron and calcium. Easy to digest and 95% digestible, tofu is an excellent weaning and geriatric food. Although made from ferment-ed soybeans, tofu does not cause flatulence, unlike beans and lentils. Is it any wonder that tofu mania is catching on everywhere?

But eating tofu as a main dish once or twice a month will not provide you with the desired health benefits. In order to take full advantage of this nutritious, disease-fighting and disease-preventing food, you must make it an integral part of your *daily* diet. The good news is that as little as 2 ounces (60 g) of tofu a day will give you the protection you need to help ward off a range of incapacitating and sometimes deadly diseases. But the challenge is: Just exactly how can you do this? How can you fully integrate tofu into your daily eating and cooking routines?

That is exactly the question I asked myself several years ago when my partner, who suffered from high cholesterol, started to become concerned about the side effects from the medication he had been on for the past five years and which, his doctor had advised him, he would have to take for the rest of his life. I had read extensively about the health benefits of tofu and other soy foods and, in particular, about soy's ability to lower "bad" cholesterol (LDL, or low density lipoprotein cholesterol), and I became determined to develop recipes containing tofu and to include tofu in my daily cooking. Five years later, I am pleased to say that my partner's cholesterol level has fallen and, although it is still above average, he no longer requires medication to keep it in check.

Unlike virtually every other tofu cookbook, *Tofu Mania* presents recipes for familiar dishes into which tofu has been incorporated. All of the recipes in this book use tofu as an *ingredient*, but very seldom is tofu the *main* ingredient. Let me give you just a quick preview of how you can cook with this versatile ingredient to reach your daily quota for optimum health. For breakfast, stir some tofu into your cereal or pancake batter. As a mid-morning snack, add tofu to your favorite muffin mix. For lunch, throw chopped tofu into your soup or substitute tofu for half the eggs in your egg salad sandwich. As a pre-dinner appetizer, you might enjoy Avocado Tofu Dip with raw vegetables. For a casual dinner, add tofu cubes to the Greek salad and to the Italian pizza or French quiche. Or, if you're throwing a dinner party, how about including tofu in the Stuffed Chicken Breasts and Alfredo sauce, as well as in the Polenta and Gingered Carrots? A classic dessert of low-fat Crème Caramel, made with tofu, of course, would be a perfect ending to this elegant dinner. These are just a few of the healthy, nutritious, low-fat recipes you will find in the following pages. Try using them as a guide to introduce tofu into your own favorite dishes.

Besides including tofu in each recipe, I have also aimed to create recipes that are healthy on other fronts—such as reducing the fat content of traditional recipes. Soft tofu, for example, is a great substitute for heavy creams generally used in rich sauces and cream soups. Wherever possible, I have reduced the egg yolk content to further decrease the cholesterol consumption. I have also cut back on the amount of meat in recipes. As you'll soon discover, by adding tofu to traditional meat recipes, you can reduce the amount of meat you would normally use while maintaining the "meaty" flavor you and your family may enjoy. The recipes in *Tofu Mania* also include wholesome ingredients such as unbleached flour, whole-wheat flour, wheat germ, grains, legumes, dried fruit, nuts, etc. For four recipes—those on pages 66, 127, 133, and 163—I provide nutritional analysis not only for my recipes, but also for the traditional recipes from which I've adapted them. Compare these analyses and discover just how much healthier it can be to cook with tofu.

Let's face it: Tofu has a reputation for being a bland food. There is a positive side to this, though, one you will quickly discover as you try the recipes in *Tofu Mania*. Tofu absorbs the flavors with which it is cooked. Throughout this book, entrée dishes are flavored with herbs, garlic and wine, and desserts get extra flavor from juice concentrates, vanilla extract and liqueurs. As a result, the recipes are delicious and healthy all-around—not just because they contain tofu.

*Tofu Mania* focuses only on tofu and not other soy foods. When I began to cook with tofu, I wanted to familiarize myself with just one soy product rather than face the challenges of experimenting with several at a time. I also realize that tofu is the most versatile soy food, and I wanted to be completely comfortable cooking with it in a wide variety of dishes. As I began making tofu a part of my daily life, I realized that I could incorporate it into literally *all* of my favorite and my family's favorite dishes. *Tofu Mania* is the result of those efforts—and I strongly believe that other cooks with little experience cooking with tofu will benefit from my focus on tofu. However, if you suffer from milk allergies, are lactose intolerant, or would simply like to increase your daily soy intake, I also highly recommend substituting soy milk for regular (cow's) milk.

It is my goal in *Tofu Mania* to demystify tofu and help you make it an everyday, healthy ingredient in your daily cooking. You need not be familiar with other cultures or become vegetarian in order to experience the multitude of health benefits offered by this miracle soy food. Go for it!

## A NOTE ABOUT THE NUTRITIONAL ANALYSIS

I have provided a nutritional analysis for every recipe. In recipes where two amounts are given, analysis is provided for the first (smaller) amount. Where alternate ingredients are given, the first listed ingredient is analyzed. Where an ingredient is optional or no specific amount is given, e.g., to taste, this ingredient is not included in the analysis. Where serving sizes vary, e.g., 4–6, the smaller portion (6) is analyzed. 2 percent milk is used in the analysis. If you substitute whole or skim milk the fat content will vary. Likewise, substituting light mayonnaise, cheese, etc., for regular products will further reduce the fat content.

These recipes were analyzed with Nutritionist IV, Version 4.1 (First Data Bank, San Bruno CA) at the University of Saskatchewan, Canada. Nutritional figures are rounded to the nearest whole number so amounts are approximate. Recipes on pages 66, 127, 133, and 163 show nutritional analysis for four traditional recipes, before they were adapted for *Tofu Mania*.

# GENERAL TIPS ON HOW TO USE AND COOK WITH TOFU

TOFU COMES IN three different textures: soft or silken, medium or regular, and firm or extra-firm.

- ■ Soft tofu is best for sauces, dips or beverages. When using soft tofu in a sauce or dip, it must be mashed or puréed to make it as smooth as possible. I generally use an electric hand blender which gives excellent results. Soft tofu is very good in fruit shakes or smoothies. It adds extra body and gives a creamy milkshake-like consistency.
- ■ Medium tofu has the most versatile texture as it is soft enough to blend or purée and firm enough to chop. It is what I use most of the time in my cooking.
- ■ To measure soft or medium tofu, place it in a glass measuring cup and, with a knife, cut it up so that it fills in the air pockets. In most recipes, the quantity of soft tofu can vary somewhat. As a rule, if the consistency of the sauce, dip or spread you are making is too thin, add a little more tofu to it; if it is too thick, add a little more liquid.

■ Firm tofu can be chopped, cubed, julienned, crumbled, puréed or grated—whatever is suitable for a particular dish. You can vary the quantity according to taste; use it as sparingly or as plentifully as you like. At first, you will probably use smaller amounts, but as you eat tofu on a regular basis, you will find yourself using it more frequently and in larger quantities—because it tastes good and is good for you!

■ Whenever a recipe calls for sour cream or whipping cream, you may substitute at least half of it with low-fat, calcium-rich tofu without sacrificing flavor.

■ Cooking with tofu enables you to reduce the fat and egg yolk (cholesterol) content used in regular recipes. I have done this whenever possible in the recipes found in this book.

■ If you do not drink milk or just want an extra dose of soy, you can substitute soy milk for regular milk in any recipe in this book. Most brands of soy milk are interchangeable with regular milk, but do check the soy milk label for confirmation. Reduced fat and fat-free soy milk are available. Some are fortified with calcium and vitamin D. Vanilla soy milk is sweet, so adjust sugar if using.

■ Tofu is available in the produce section of most supermarkets. It comes packed either in water in plastic containers or in vacuum-packed cartons. Both types must be refrigerated after opening. The water-packed variety will stay fresh about one week if the water is changed daily. Before purchasing, check the expiration date.

# AT A GLANCE ... HOW TO USE TOFU IN YOUR OWN FAVORITE RECIPES

ADD MEDIUM OR firm tofu (chopped, cubed, julienned, crumbled, puréed or grated) to:

- burgers (meat, fish or vegetarian)
- casseroles
- pizza toppings
- salads
- sandwiches (including pita pockets, fajitas, etc.)
- soups
- chilis
- stews
- stir-fries

Use mashed or puréed soft or medium tofu in:

- beverages
- dips
- spreads
- salad dressings
- gravies
- sauces
- homemade pastas
- custards
- puddings
- creams
- toppings
- muffin batter
- pancake batter
- cake batter
- yeast dough

**Note:** Crumbled firm or medium tofu tends to disappear into salads, chilies, stews, stir-fries, etc. Rather than cubing tofu in these recipes, you may prefer to crumble or grate it so that it becomes a more integral part of the recipe.

## COMPOSITION AND NUTRIENT VALUE OF TOFU PER 100 GRAMS

TOFU, REGULAR, RAW MADE WITH CALCIUM SULPHATE: 76 Kilocalorie, 84.6% water, 8.1 g Protein, 1.9 g Carbohydrate, 4.8 g Total Fat, 0.69 g Total Saturated Fatty Acid, 1.06 g Monounsaturated Fatty Acid, 2.70 g Polyunsaturated Fatty Acid, 0 mg Cholesterol, 2.38 g Linoleic Acid, 0.73 g Total Dietary Fiber, 9 RE Vitamin A, 0.08 mg Thiamin (Vitamin $B_1$), 0.05 mg Riboflavin (Vitamin $B_2$), 2.3 NE Total Niacin Equivalent, 0.047 mg Pyridoxine (Vitamin $B_6$), 0 pg Cabalanim (Vitamin $B_12$), 15.0 pg Folacin (Folic Acid), 0.1 mg Vitamin C (Ascorbic Acid), 30 mg Magnesium, 350 mg Calcium, 97 mg Phosphorus, 5.36 mg Iron, 0.80 mg Zinc, 121 mg Potassium, 7 mg Sodium, 0.193 mg Copper, 0.605 mg Manganese.

# BREAKFAST, BRUNCH, AND LUNCH

# Cream of Wheat

START THE DAY with this nutritious, low-fat hot cereal and you won't experience hunger pangs halfway through the morning.

| | |
|---|---|
| 1 cup | milk |
| ½ cup | soft *or* medium tofu |
| ½ cup | water |
| 2 tbsp. | raisins |
| ⅓ cup | Cream of Wheat cereal |
| 1 tbsp. | maple syrup |
| | cinnamon and sugar, for sprinkling |

In a small saucepan, using an electric hand blender, blend together milk, tofu, and water. Over medium-high heat, bring mixture to a boil. Stir in raisins and cereal. Reduce heat to low and let simmer about 3 minutes. (If mixture is too thick, add a little milk or water and return to a boil.) Remove from heat and stir in maple syrup. Serve sprinkled with cinnamon and sugar.

Serves 2

PER SERVING: 147 calories, 6 g protein, 24 g carbohydrate, 3 g total fat (1 g saturated fat, 1 g mono, 1 g poly fat), 9 mg cholesterol, 1 g dietary fiber, 70 RE vitamin A, 7 mcg folate, 2 mg vitamin C, 67 mg sodium, 279 mg potassium, 2 mg iron, 180 mg calcium

**Variations:**

You can add tofu to other cereals (e.g., oatmeal, Muesli) in the same way as above.

# Tofu Fruit Shakes

**THESE REFRESHING, HEALTHY** shakes are a low-fat alternative to regular ice-cream shakes. They can be made with any fruit or combination of fruits. The following is one of my favorites.

### Banana Strawberry Shake

|        |                            |
| ------ | -------------------------- |
| 2      | ice cubes                  |
| ½ cup  | soft tofu                  |
| ½      | lemon, juice of            |
| ½      | banana                     |
| 1 cup  | fresh strawberries         |
|        | honey *or* maple syrup, to taste |

Combine all ingredients in a blender. Process until smooth. If the shake is too thick, add a little soy or regular milk.

Makes 1, 2–cup shake or 2, 1–cup shakes

> PER CUP: 69 calories, 2 g protein, 14 g carbohydrate, 1 g total fat (trace saturated fat, trace mono, 1 g poly fat), 0 mg cholesterol, 2 g dietary fiber, 5 RE vitamin A, 21 mcg folate, 52 mg vitamin C, 3 mg sodium, 255 mg potassium, 1 mg iron, 20 mg calcium

**Variations:**

Try sliced peaches, nectarines, mangos, raspberries, blueberries, kiwis, oranges, pineapple instead of strawberries and/or bananas. Additional flavorings could include cinnamon, nutmeg, almond, vanilla or coconut extracts.

Delicious combinations are:

- mangoes
  blueberries
- peaches
  raspberries
- mangoes
  raspberries
- kiwis
  nectarines

- nectarines
  strawberries
- bananas
  peaches
- oranges
  bananas
- crushed pineapple
  piña colada or
  coconut extract flavoring

# French Toast

HALF THE EGGS, same luscious flavor as regular French toast!

|   |   |
|---|---|
| 4 | eggs |
| I cup | soft tofu |
| pinch | salt |
| ¼ cup | milk |
| 8 slices | bread, regular *or* Italian-style |

In a medium bowl, with a hand blender, blend together eggs, tofu, salt, and milk. Dip bread slices, 2 at a time, into egg mixture, and let soak 1 to 2 minutes.

In a lightly greased frying pan, over medium heat, fry bread slices about 2 minutes per side, or until golden brown. Repeat with remaining bread slices.

Serve immediately with maple syrup and sliced fresh fruits or berries.

Serves 4

PER SERVING: 221 calories, 12 g protein, 24 g carbohydrate, 8 g total fat (2 g saturated fat, 3 g mono, 2 g poly fat), 213 mg cholesterol, 1 g dietary fiber, 104 RE vitamin A, 40 mcg folate, trace vitamin C, 308 mg sodium, 136 mg potassium, 2 mg iron, 108 mg calcium

**Variations:**

For a sweeter version, add 1 to 2 tbsp. maple syrup or sugar and 1 tsp. vanilla to the egg mixture. Toast can also be dusted with icing (confectioner's) sugar before serving.

# Crêpes

HOWEVER YOU SERVE these versatile crêpes—simply rolled up with maple syrup or jam or as stuffed manicotti or fajitas—they always garner raves.

| | |
|---:|:---|
| I cup | soft tofu |
| 2 | eggs |
| I | egg white |
| I ½ cups | milk |
| I cup | water |
| I tbsp. | vegetable oil |
| I ½ cups | unbleached flour |
| ½ tsp. | salt |

In a large bowl, using an electric hand blender, blend together tofu, eggs, and egg white. Beat in remaining ingredients until mixture is smooth and creamy

Heat a lightly greased nonstick frying pan. When hot, pour enough batter to thinly coat bottom of pan. Tilt the pan in a quick, circular motion to spread the batter evenly. Cook over medium-high heat, about 30 to 40 seconds per side. Crêpes should be very thin.

Stack crêpes to prevent them from drying out. Serve immediately or cover and refrigerate until ready to use, up to 2 days.

Makes about 20, 8-inch crêpes

> PER CRÊPE: 63 calories, 3 g protein, 9 g carbohydrate, 2 g total fat (trace saturated fat, I g mono, trace poly fat), 23 mg cholesterol, 0 g dietary fiber, 20 RE vitamin A, 3 mcg folate, trace vitamin C, 77 mg sodium, 47 mg potassium, trace iron, 27 mg calcium

**Variations:**

For **dessert crêpes**, you can add 1 to 2 tbsp. of sugar and decrease the salt to ¼ tsp.

# Breakfast Muffins

EVERYONE WILL ENJOY these moist, "packed-with-goodness" muffins.

| | |
|---|---|
| 1 cup | unbleached flour |
| ¼ cup | rolled oats |
| ¼ cup | wheat bran |
| 1 tsp. | baking powder |
| 1 tsp. | baking soda |
| pinch | salt |
| ¾ cup | brown sugar |
| ½ tsp. | cinnamon |
| ⅛ tsp. | ground cloves |
| ¾ cup | soft *or* medium tofu |
| 1 | egg |
| ½ tsp. | vanilla extract |
| 3 tbsp. | vegetable oil |
| 14 oz. | can crushed pineapple, drained |
| ½ cup | grated carrots |
| ¼ cup | raisins |

Preheat oven to 400°F. Lightly grease 12 muffin cups.

In a large bowl, combine first 9 (dry) ingredients.

In a medium bowl, whisk together tofu, egg, vanilla, and oil. Fold in pineapple, carrots, and raisins. Add to dry ingredients and stir just until combined. Spoon batter into muffin cups.

Bake 17 to 20 minutes, or until toothpick inserted in center comes out clean.

Makes 12 muffins

PER MUFFIN: 164 calories, 3 g protein, 30 g carbohydrate, 4 g total fat (1 g saturated fat, 2 g mono, 2 g poly fat), 18 mg cholesterol, 1 g dietary fiber, 140 RE vitamin A, 6 mcg folate, 3 mg vitamin C, 149 mg sodium, 165 mg potassium, 1 mg iron, 57 mg calcium

# Cherry Pancakes

THESE SCRUMPTIOUS PANCAKES have no added fat whatsoever!

|        |                                                        |
|-------:|--------------------------------------------------------|
| 2      | eggs                                                   |
| ½ cup  | soft *or* medium tofu                                  |
| ½ cup  | cherry juice (from frozen *or* canned cherries) *or* buttermilk |
| I cup  | unbleached flour                                       |
| ½ tsp. | baking powder                                          |
| I½ tbsp. | sugar                                                |
| 2 cups | pitted sour cherries (fresh, canned *or* thawed) sugar for sprinkling |

In a medium bowl, with a hand blender, blend together eggs, tofu, and cherry juice. Mix in flour, baking powder and 1½ tbsp. sugar. Batter should be thick and smooth. Fold in cherries.

To cook pancakes, heat a lightly greased nonstick frying pan over medium heat. Drop large spoonfuls of batter into pan, spreading the mixture so that each pancake is about 2½ inches in diameter. Fry 2 minutes per side, or until lightly browned. Transfer to a serving platter and sprinkle generously with sugar.

Makes 18 to 20, 2½-inch pancakes

> PER PANCAKE: 48 calories, 2 g protein, 9 g carbohydrate, 1 g total fat (trace saturated fat, trace mono, trace poly fat), 21 mg cholesterol, .2 g dietary fiber, 29 RE vitamin A, 4 mcg folate, 3 mg vitamin C, 16 mg sodium, 45 mg potassium, .4 mg iron, 15 mg calcium

**Variations:**

For **Blueberry**, **Peach**, or **Apple Pancakes**, substitute equal quantities of blueberries or chopped peaches or apples.

# Baking Powder Biscuits

THE QUICKEST WAY to have home-baked rolls is to make biscuits—and these take just minutes to prepare. They are good at any time of the day, with meals or as a snack.

### Plain Biscuits

| | |
|---|---|
| 2½ cups | unbleached flour |
| 4 tsp. | baking powder |
| 1 tsp. | salt |
| ¼ cup | butter |
| ½ cup | puréed soft tofu |
| ⅔ cup | milk |

Preheat oven to 400°F.

In a medium bowl, combine flour, baking powder and salt. Mix in butter with a pastry blender until mixture is evenly crumbly. Stir in tofu and milk. Knead a few seconds on a lightly floured board, until dough is soft. Roll or pat to approximately ¾" thickness. Cut with a 2" cookie cutter and place rounds on ungreased cookie sheet about 1" apart.

Bake 18 to 20 minutes. Serve warm.

Makes 12 to 14 biscuits

PER BISCUIT: 125 calories, 3 g protein, 19 g carbohydrate, 4 g total fat (2 g saturated fat, 1 g mono, trace poly fat), 10 mg cholesterol, 0 g dietary fiber, 39 RE vitamin A, 1 mcg folate, trace vitamin C, 311 mg sodium, 43 mg potassium, 1 mg iron, 113 mg calcium

NOTE: Leftover biscuits taste best when reheated, either in a conventional oven for a firm crust or in a microwave oven for a soft crust.

# Hearty Biscuits

THE ROLLED OATS and whole wheat flour make these a heartier alternative to plain biscuits—and the perfect accompaniment to hearty soups such as **Leek and Potato** (p. 72) or **Winter Vegetable** (p. 73).

| | |
|---|---|
| 1½ cups | unbleached flour |
| ¼ cup | rolled oats |
| 2 tbsp. | whole-wheat flour |
| 4 tsp. | baking powder |
| 1 tsp. | salt |
| ¼ cup | butter |
| ½ cup | mashed soft tofu |
| ⅔ cup | milk |

Proceed as for plain biscuits.

Makes 12 to 14 biscuits.

PER BISCUIT: 100 calories, 3 g protein, 13 g carbohydrate, 4 g total fat (2 g saturated fat, 1 g mono, trace poly fat), 10 mg cholesterol, .2 g dietary fiber, 39 RE vitamin A, 1 mcg folate, trace vitamin C, 311 mg sodium, 39 mg potassium, 1 mg iron, 114 mg calcium

**Variations for either the plain or hearty recipe:**

- *Cinnamon Raisin Biscuits.* Add ½ tsp. ground cinnamon and 3 tbsp. sugar to the flour mixture. Before adding tofu and milk, mix in ⅔ cup raisins.
- *Cheese Biscuits.* Mix in ⅔ cup shredded Cheddar, Monterey Jack, or Swiss cheese before adding tofu and milk, *or* ½ cup grated Parmesan cheese.
- *Peppery Cheese Biscuits.* Add ½ tsp. (or to taste) dried red pepper flakes *or* ¼ cup chopped jalapeño pepper to Cheese Biscuits.
- *Herb Biscuits.* Mix in 2 to 3 tbsp. of your favorite chopped fresh herbs, such as dill, sage, basil, rosemary, chives or a combination of two or three of them.
- *Sun-Dried Tomato and/or Olive Biscuits.* Add 5 to 6 tbsp. finely chopped sun-dried tomatoes and/or 2 to 3 tbsp. chopped black Italian or Greek olives.

# Cinnamon Raisin Doughnuts

HEALTHY INGREDIENTS AND quick and easy preparation combine to make these "crisp-on-the-outside, doughy-on-the-inside" pastries a satisfying treat. Great for brunch or as a mid-morning or afternoon snack.

| | |
|---:|:---|
| ½ cup | buttermilk |
| 1 | egg |
| 1 | egg white |
| 1⅓ cups | unbleached flour |
| ½ cup | wheat germ |
| 1 tbsp. | baking powder |
| ⅓ cup | granulated sugar |
| ½–1 tsp. | cinnamon |
| dash | salt |
| ½ cup | raisins |
| 1 cup | grated extra-firm tofu |
| | oil for frying (enough to cover doughnuts) |
| | sugar for sprinkling |

In a large bowl, whisk together buttermilk, egg, and egg white. Add the next 8 ingredients. Mix until smooth and shape into a ball.

Roll out dough on floured board to approximately ½ inch in thickness. (Dough may be sticky, so sprinkle board and dough with a little more flour as needed.) With a 3½-inch cookie cutter, cut out rounds. Using a thimble or apple corer, cut out centers.

When all the dough is used up, heat oil to 365°F in wok or deep frying pan. Fry doughnuts in batches of 5 or 6 for 2 to 3 minutes per side. When lightly browned, remove doughnuts from oil and drain on paper towels. Generously sprinkle them with sugar. Transfer doughnuts to a serving platter.

Makes 18 to 20, 3½-inch doughnuts

PER DOUGHNUT: 83 calories, 4 g protein, 15 g carbohydrate, 1 g total fat (trace saturated fat, trace mono, 1 g poly fat), 11 mg cholesterol, 1 g dietary fiber, 10 RE vitamin A, 12 mcg folate, 1 mg vitamin C, 64 mg sodium, 79 mg potassium, 1 mg iron, 63 mg calcium

# Dried Fruit Loaf

A WONDERFUL ALTERNATIVE to traditional fruit cake, this wholesome and flavorful fruit loaf is definitely intended for the health-conscious gourmet. This recipe calls for only 2 eggs and no added fat.

| | |
|---|---|
| ¾ cup | unbleached flour |
| ¼ tsp. | baking soda |
| ¼ tsp. | baking powder |
| ½ tsp. | salt |
| ¾ cup | brown sugar |
| 1 cup | dried apricot halves |
| 1 cup | coarsely chopped dates |
| 1½ cups | chopped mixed dried fruit such as pears, apples, raisins, cherries, prunes, cranberries, figs |
| 1 cup | pecan *or* walnut halves |
| 1 cup | slivered almonds |
| 2 | eggs |
| 1 tsp. | vanilla extract |
| ½–¾ cup | soft tofu, depending on dryness of fruit |

Preheat oven to 300°F. Lightly grease a 5 x 9" nonstick loaf pan, or line pan with waxed paper, for easy removal.

Pour flour, baking soda, baking powder, salt, and brown sugar into a large mixing bowl. Using fingers, mix in dried fruit and nuts. Set aside.

In a small bowl, beat eggs, vanilla, and tofu until smooth. Fold into dry ingredients until fruit and nuts are evenly coated. Pour into pan, pressing down to avoid air pockets.

Bake 1 hour 15 minutes to 1 hour 30 minutes. Let sit 5 minutes before removing loaf from pan. Cool on wire rack. Cut into thin slices and spread with a little butter. Delicious!

Makes 1, 5 x 9" loaf, 20 to 24 servings

PER SERVING: 131 calories, 2 g protein, 18 g carbohydrate, 7 g total fat (1 g saturated fat, 4 g mono, 1 g poly fat), 18 mg cholesterol, 2 g dietary fiber, 48 RE vitamin A, 9 mcg folate, trace vitamin C, 119 mg sodium, 214 mg potassium, 1 mg iron, 35 mg calcium

# Holiday Cranberry-Apricot Soda Bread

YOU'D LIKE TO bake something for Christmas or Easter morning, but with all the preparations yet to be done you just don't have the time. Well, this wholesome bread takes only 15 minutes to prepare and less than 1 hour to bake. Maybe you'll try it, after all! It's also perfect for a weekend brunch.

| | |
|---|---|
| 2½ cups | unbleached flour |
| ½ cup | rolled oats |
| 2 tbsp. | granulated sugar |
| 1½ tsp. | baking soda |
| ½ tsp. | salt |
| ¼ cup | butter, at room temperature |
| ⅔ cup | chopped hazelnuts *or* pecans |
| ⅔ cup | dried cranberries *or* dried Bing cherries |
| ⅓ cup | chopped dried apricots |
| ⅓ cup | raisins |
| 1 cup | soft tofu |
| ½ cup | buttermilk *or* milk |
| | sugar for sprinkling |

Preheat oven to 375°F.

In a large bowl, combine flour, oats, sugar, baking soda, and salt. Cut in butter; mix into flour mixture with a pastry blender. When evenly crumbly, add hazelnuts, cranberries, apricots, and raisins.

In a small bowl, using a hand blender, blend together tofu and buttermilk. Mix into dry ingredients. On a floured board, knead dough until fairly smooth. If too sticky, add a little flour.

Shape dough into a ball and place on a lightly greased baking sheet. Flatten slightly and cut a large **X** in the top. Sprinkle with sugar.

Bake 50 to 60 minutes, or until lightly browned and a toothpick inserted in the center comes out clean. Cool on a wire rack.

Makes 1 loaf, about 10 servings

PER SERVING: 274 calories, 7 g protein, 39 g carbohydrate, 11 g total fat (3 g saturated fat, 5 g mono, 1 g poly fat), 13 mg cholesterol, 2 g dietary fiber, 89 RE vitamin A, 13 mcg folate, 3 mg vitamin C, 360 mg sodium, 206 mg potassium, 2 mg iron, 29 mg calcium

# Multigrain Health Bread

**THIS WHOLESOME BREAD** has it all—lots of fiber, great texture, and flavor, yet it contains no cholesterol and is almost fat free. I love it!

| | |
|---|---|
| ½ cup | rolled oats |
| ½ cup | mixed grain cereal (such as cracked wheat, cracked rye, flaxseed, cornmeal, etc.) |
| 2 cups | boiling water |
| 5 tsp. | honey, divided |
| ½ cup | warm water |
| 2 tbsp. | active dry yeast (2 pkgs.) |
| 1 tbsp. | salt |
| 1 cup | puréed soft *or* medium tofu |
| 1 cup | whole-wheat flour |
| 3½-4½ cups | unbleached flour (depending on dryness of flour and cereals) |
| ¼ cup | chopped walnuts *or* pecans |

In a large bowl, combine oats, cereals and water. Let soak.

Meanwhile, in a small bowl, dissolve 2 tsp. honey in warm water. Add yeast and let stand 10 minutes, or until yeast is bubbly, then stir. Fold into cereal mixture. Add remaining 3 tsp. honey, salt, and puréed tofu. Gradually blend in flour, 1 cup at a time, to make a soft dough. Mix in nuts. Turn onto a floured board; knead until smooth and elastic, about 5 minutes. Form into a ball; place in a greased bowl, turning to grease top. Cover; let rise in warm place, free from draft, until doubled in bulk, about 1 hour.

Turn dough out onto floured board. Punch dough down. Cover and let rest about 10 minutes. Cut dough in half and shape into 2 loaves. Place in greased loaf pans; cover and let rise again until doubled in bulk, about 1 hour. Bake at 400°F about 30 to 35 minutes. Remove bread from pans and cool completely on wire racks before cutting.

Makes 2, 3 x 5 x 9" loaves, 24 servings

PER SERVING: 114 calories, 4 g protein, 22 g carbohydrate, 1 g total fat (trace saturated fat, trace g mono, trace g poly fat), 0 mg cholesterol, 1 g dietary fiber, 3 RE vitamin A, 26 mcg folate, trace vitamin C, 297 mg sodium, 58 mg potassium, 1 mg iron, 5 mg calcium

# Honey Twist

ABOUT ONCE A month my daughter Lara reminds me that it is time to bake another Honey Twist—her very favorite coffee bread and mine, too. Yeast breads take a little longer to prepare than quick breads, which are made with baking powder, but they are well worth the effort. Is there anything more inviting than the aroma of freshly baked yeast bread? For this bread I use a deep oval casserole.

| | |
|---:|---|
| 1 cup | milk, scalded |
| ¼ cup | butter |
| ½ cup | sugar |
| 1 tsp. | salt |
| ¼ cup | lukewarm water |
| 1 tsp. | sugar |
| 2 tbsp. | active dry yeast (2 pkgs.) |
| 3 | eggs |
| 1 cup | soft tofu |
| 1 | lemon, zest of, grated |
| 5–6 cups | unbleached flour |

In a large bowl, pour hot milk over butter, ½ cup sugar, and salt. Pour luke-warm water into a small bowl. Stir in 1 tsp. sugar and yeast. Let stand 10 minutes, or until yeast is bubbly, then stir.

In a small separate bowl, combine eggs and tofu, using a whisk or hand blender, until smooth.

When milk in the large bowl has cooled to lukewarm, add yeast, egg and tofu mixture, and lemon zest, stirring gently. Gradually blend in flour to make a soft dough. Turn out onto floured board and knead until smooth and elastic, about 5 minutes. Form into a ball and place in greased bowl, turning to grease top. Cover and let rise in warm place, free from draft, until doubled in bulk, about 1 hour.

Shape dough into long roll about 1" in diameter. Coil roll in an overlapping fashion into a greased oval 9 x 14" casserole, beginning at the outside. Brush with Honey Topping (recipe follows). Let rise until doubled in bulk, about 1 hour.

Bake at 375°F about 30 minutes, or until lightly browned. Remove from pan. Be sure to cool Honey Twist at least 30 minutes on wire rack before cutting into it.

### Honey Topping

| | |
|---|---|
| **2 tbsp.** | **melted butter** |
| **½ cup** | **sugar** |
| **3 tbsp.** | **honey** |
| **I** | **egg white** |

Combine all ingredients until smooth. Brush over twist before second rising.

Makes 1 large oval coffee bread (9 x 14″), 20 to 24 servings

PER SERVING: 189 calories, 5 g protein, 32 g carbohydrate, 4 g total fat (2 g saturated fat, I g mono, trace poly fat), 35 mg cholesterol, trace dietary fiber, 46 RE vitamin A, 27 mcg folate, I mg vitamin C, 144 mg sodium, 77 mg potassium, I mg iron, 19 mg calcium

# Mediterranean Pizza

This pizza is the #1 favorite in our family. We love the fresh, full-bodied Mediterranean flavors created by cooking tomatoes, onions, artichokes, olives, and herbs together. Try it! It may become your favorite pizza, too.

**12" pizza crust (p. 36)**

### Toppings

| | |
|---|---|
| I | medium tomato, thinly sliced |
| I | medium onion, halved and thinly sliced |
| 4–6 | cooked artichoke hearts, quartered |
| ½-¾ cup | cubed medium tofu |
| 2 tbsp. | crumbled feta *or* goat cheese |
| 4 | sun-dried tomatoes, in oil, drained, coarsely chopped |
| 2 tbsp. | sliced olives |
| | generous pinch *each*, dried oregano and tarragon |
| 4–6 | mushrooms, sliced |
| | salt and pepper, to taste |
| 2 tbsp. | grated Parmesan |
| ½ cup | shredded mozzarella *or* Swiss cheese |

Preheat oven to 425°F. Layer toppings on pizza crust in the order listed above. Bake 12 to 15 minutes, or until crust is golden.

Makes 1, 12-inch pizza, 8 servings

PER SLICE: 274 calories, 11 g protein, 33 g carbohydrate, 13 g total fat (3 g saturated fat, 7 g mono, 2 g poly fat), 8 mg cholesterol, 5 g dietary fiber, 83 RE vitamin A, 70 mcg folate, 35 mg vitamin C, 353 mg sodium, 707 mg potassium, 4 mg iron, 153 mg calcium

**Variations:**

Pizza toppings are limited only by your imagination. If you want to use a tomato sauce, spread it evenly over the crust and layer toppings. Topping ideas can include spinach, fresh or roasted red and green peppers, minced garlic, bacon, sausage, pepperoni, shrimp, scallops, clams, red pepper flakes, basil, rosemary, thyme, or sage. Sliced cooked potatoes, drizzled with olive oil and a sprinkle of rosemary or sage, salt, and pepper to taste are a delicious combination. Always add grated or cubed tofu to your cheese topping.

# Pizza Crust

NO RISING TIME makes this pizza crust ideal for people on the run. It takes just under 30 minutes to get it ready for the oven.

| | |
|---|---|
| 1 tsp. | cornmeal |
| 1 tsp. | honey |
| ½ cup | warm water |
| 1 tbsp. | active dry yeast (1 pkg.) |
| 1 cup | unbleached flour |
| ½ cup | whole-wheat flour |
| ¼ tsp. | salt |
| ¼ cup | grated firm tofu |
| 2 tbsp. | olive oil |

Preheat oven to 425°F. Lightly grease a 12″ pizza pan. Sprinkle it with cornmeal.

In a small bowl, dissolve honey in warm water. Add yeast and let sit about 10 minutes, or until yeast is bubbly.

In a medium bowl, mix flours, salt, and tofu. Add yeast and oil. Knead until smooth, 5 to 8 minutes. Dough will be firm.

Roll out dough to fit into pizza pan. Add your favorite toppings, including tofu, of course!

Bake about 15 minutes.

Makes 1, 12-inch pizza, 8 servings

> PER SLICE: 136 calories, 4 g protein, 20 g carbohydrate, 4 g total fat (trace saturated fat, 3 g mono, 1 g poly fat), 0 mg cholesterol, 1 g dietary fiber, 1 RE vitamin A, 40 mcg folate, trace vitamin C, 75 mg sodium, 73 mg potassium, 2 mg iron, 19 mg calcium

NOTE: For a thicker breadlike crust let pizza rise 30 minutes before baking it.

# Onion Bacon Quiche

**THE BACON ADDS** to the flavor of the quiche but if you prefer, leave it out and sauté the onions in 1 tbsp. vegetable oil.

|          | pastry for 9" single pie crust (p. 167) |
|---------:|:----------------------------------------|
| 5        | slices raw bacon, chopped               |
| 2 cups   | finely chopped sweet onions             |
| ¼ tsp.   | caraway seeds                           |
| ¼ cup    | soft tofu                               |
| ¼ cup    | plain yogurt *or* sour cream            |
| 2        | eggs                                    |
| 2 tbsp.  | unripened goat cheese                   |
| 1 tbsp.  | flour                                   |
| ½ cup    | cubed medium *or* firm tofu             |
| ¼ tsp.   | dried tarragon                          |
|          | salt and pepper, to taste               |

Line a greased pie plate with rolled out pastry.

Preheat oven to 350°F.

In a medium frying pan, over medium-high heat, cook bacon about 2 minutes. Add onions and caraway seeds. Reduce heat to medium. Cook onions until translucent, about 5 to 8 minutes, stirring occasionally. Remove from heat.

In a medium bowl, using a hand blender, blend together soft tofu, yogurt, eggs, and goat cheese. Fold in flour, onions and bacon, cubed tofu, tarragon, and seasonings. Pour into prepared pie shell.

Bake 45 to 50 minutes, or until custard is set and crust is light golden.

Makes 1, 9-inch quiche, 6 to 8 servings

PER SLICE: 202 calories, 8 g protein, 17 g carbohydrate, 12 g total fat (5 g saturated fat, 3 g mono, 1 g poly fat), 77 mg cholesterol, 1 g dietary fiber, 88 RE vitamin A, 18 mcg folate, 4 mg vitamin C, 293 mg sodium, 156 mg potassium, 2 mg iron, 73 mg calcium

# French Onion Pie

A WONDERFULLY SOFT biscuit-like crust and a topping packed with flavor make this a delicious choice any time. If you like the crust, use it as a base for pizzas, quiches and other pies. A word about the garlic: According to a Pennsylvania State University study, garlic's healing powers develop after it is peeled, so peel the garlic cloves and let them sit for about 15 minutes before using them in cooking.

## Crust

| | |
|---|---|
| 2 cups | unbleached flour |
| ¼ cup | cornmeal |
| 1½ tbsp. | baking powder |
| 1 tsp. | salt |
| ½ cup | mashed soft tofu |
| ¼ cup | milk |
| ¼ cup | vegetable oil |

## Topping

| | |
|---|---|
| 4 | slices raw bacon, chopped |
| 4 cups | sliced onions |
| 2 tsp. | dried herbes de Provence, divided (see p. 99) |
| 3 oz. | can flat anchovy fillets, divided |
| 2–3 | garlic cloves, minced |
| 18 | Kalamata olives (or other), pitted |
| 2 | sun-dried tomatoes, in oil, drained |
| ½ cup | grated firm tofu |
| 2 tbsp. | grated Parmesan cheese |
| 1 | ripe tomato, thinly sliced |
| ¼ cup | shredded Swiss cheese |

**TO MAKE CRUST:** Combine flour, cornmeal, baking powder, and salt in a medium bowl. Set aside.

In a small bowl, using a hand blender, blend together tofu and milk. Add oil. Stir into flour mixture. Knead just until dough sticks together. Pat dough into a ball. Place on a wooden board and cover with a sheet of waxed paper.

Roll out dough to fit lightly greased pizza pan. Remove waxed paper. Roll up edges of dough.

**TO MAKE TOPPING:** In a large skillet, over high heat, sauté bacon 1 minute. Fold in onions and ½ of herbs. Reduce heat to low and simmer 20 to 30 minutes, stirring occasionally. Onions should be very soft. Remove from heat.

Preheat oven to 400°F.

Combine 3 anchovies, garlic, 12 olives, and sun-dried tomatoes in a food processor. Pulse until mixture resembles a coarse paste. Fold in grated tofu. Using a spatula, spread paste evenly over crust. Sprinkle with Parmesan.

Spread remaining toppings as follows: cooked onions, tomato slices, remaining anchovies and olives, and the Swiss cheese. Sprinkle with the remaining herbs.

Bake 20 to 25 minutes, or until crust is golden and toppings are bubbly. Let sit 5 minutes before cutting into it.

Makes 1, 12-inch pie, 8 servings

PER SLICE: 356 calories, 14 g protein, 40 g carbohydrate, 16 g total fat (3 g saturated fat, 6 g mono, 5 g poly fat), 17 mg cholesterol, 3 g dietary fiber, 48 RE vitamin A, 28 mcg folate, 16 mg vitamin C, 1155 mg sodium, 435 mg potassium, 4 mg iron, 334 mg calcium

# Grilled Quesadillas

**EASY TO PREPARE**, nutritious yet light, grilled quesadillas are delicious for lunch or dinner. If desired, they can be pan fried instead of grilled.

| | |
|---:|:---|
| 8 | **8" flour tortillas** |
| 14 oz. | **can refried beans** |
| 2 | **ripe Roma tomatoes, diced** |
| 2 | **green onions, thinly sliced** |
| 1 | **large garlic clove, minced** |
| 1 tbsp. | *each*, **chopped fresh parsley and basil** |
| 2 tbsp. | **olive oil, divided** |
| 1 tbsp. | **balsamic vinegar** |
| | **salt and pepper, to taste** |
| 1 cup | **cubed medium *or* firm tofu** |
| 1 cup | **grated Cheddar *or* mozzarella cheese** |

Spread half of each tortilla with refried beans.

In a large bowl, combine tomatoes, onions, garlic, parsley, basil, 1 tbsp. oil, vinegar, salt, and pepper. Fold in tofu.

Spread mixture evenly over refried beans. Sprinkle with cheese. Fold uncovered half of tortilla over filling and press edges together. Brush both sides with remaining oil.

Grill (or pan fry) over medium heat, 2 to 4 minutes on each side, or until filling is heated through and quesadillas are lightly browned.

Serves 8

**Variations:**

If you'd like some meat in your quesadillas, substitute ½ cup thin strips of cooked chicken or beef for ½ cup tofu.

PER QUESADILLA: 280 calories, 12 g protein, 30 g carbohydrate, 13 g total fat (4 g saturated fat, 5 g mono, 2 g poly fat), 19 mg cholesterol, 5 g dietary fiber, 69 RE vitamin A, 23 mcg folate, 10 mg vitamin C, 409 mg sodium, 310 mg potassium, 4 mg iron, 200 mg calcium

# Grilled Cheese Sandwiches

ADD TOFU AND onions to your grilled cheese sandwiches next time you make them. It's a winning combination.

|          | butter                      |
|----------|-----------------------------|
| 4 slices | bread                       |
| 2 slices | cheese                      |
| ¼ cup    | grated firm tofu            |
| 1        | green onion, thinly sliced  |

Butter outside of each bread slice. Layer the cheese, tofu, and onion between the bread slices. Lightly brown each side of the sandwiches in a non-stick pan or sandwich maker.

Makes 2 sandwiches

PER SANDWICH: 279 calories, 15 g protein, 25 g carbohydrate, 14 g total fat (7 g saturated fat, 4 g mono, 2 g poly fat), 30 mg cholesterol, 2 g dietary fiber, 127 RE vitamin A, 27 mcg folate, 1 mg vitamin C, 401 mg sodium, 135 mg potassium, 5 mg iron, 325 mg calcium

# Tuna or Salmon Sandwiches or Wraps

| | |
|---|---|
| 7½ oz. | can tuna *or* salmon, drained |
| ⅓ cup | medium tofu |
| 2–3 tbsp. | mayonnaise, or to taste |
| | pepper, to taste |
| 1 | green onion, thinly sliced |
| 6 slices | bread *or* 3, 8" flour tortillas |
| | sprouts or spinach leaves (optional) |

Mash fish, tofu, and mayonnaise together in a small bowl. Fold in pepper and onion. Spread mixture on 3 bread slices. Top with sprouts or spinach leaves and remaining bread slices *or* spread filling on tortillas, add toppings, and wrap.

Makes 3 sandwiches or wraps

PER SANDWICH: 300 calories, 24 g protein, 25 g carbohydrate, 11 g total fat (2 g saturated fat, 1 g mono, 7 g poly fat), 28 mg cholesterol, 2 g dietary fiber, 15 RE vitamin A, 24 mcg folate, trace vitamin C, 550 mg sodium, 262 mg potassium, 4 mg iron, 102 mg calcium

# Tuna Melts

THESE MELTS CAN be made with other canned seafood, such as crab or salmon. They make a healthy light lunch.

| | |
|---:|---|
| 4 slices | Italian-type bread |
| 7.5 oz. | can tuna, drained |
| 1 | celery stalk, finely chopped |
| ½ | medium onion, finely chopped |
| 1 tbsp. | chopped fresh dill |
| ½ cup | grated firm tofu |
| 2–3 tbsp. | mayonnaise |
| | pepper, to taste |
| 1 tsp. | Dijon mustard |
| 4 slices | light mozzarella cheese |

Preheat oven to broil.

Toast bread slices. Arrange them on a baking dish. Combine next 8 ingredients and spread thickly on toast. Top with cheese slices. Broil 5 minutes, or until cheese is bubbly and golden. Turn off oven and let sit 5 minutes before serving.

Makes 4 open-faced sandwiches

PER SANDWICH: 320 calories, 28 g protein, 19 g carbohydrate, 14 g total fat (5 g saturated fat, 2 g mono, 6 g poly fat), 37 mg cholesterol, 2 g dietary fiber, 67 RE vitamin A, 29 mcg folate, 2 mg vitamin C, 544 mg sodium, 313 mg potassium, 5 mg iron, 286 mg calcium

# Egg Salad

YOU'D NEVER KNOW there was tofu in this egg salad mixture! Perfect either as a salad or as a filling for sandwiches, it tastes exactly like traditional egg salad, but it's made with half the eggs, therefore half the cholesterol!

|  |  |
|---|---|
| 4 | hard-boiled eggs, chopped |
| I cup | grated firm tofu |
| I | small onion, finely chopped |
| ¼ cup | mayonnaise, or to taste |
| I tsp. | Dijon mustard |
|  | salt and pepper, to taste |

Combine all ingredients. Use as a spread for egg salad sandwiches. Keep refrigerated.

Makes 2 cups, 4 servings

PER SANDWICH: 270 calories, 17 g protein, 5 g carbohydrate, 22 g total fat (4 g saturated fat, 3 g mono, 10 g poly fat), 222 mg cholesterol, 2 g dietary fiber, 95 RE vitamin A, 44 mcg folate, 1 mg vitamin C, 154 mg sodium, 246 mg potassium, 7 mg iron, 160 mg calcium

**Variations:**

Add 1 tbsp. of chopped capers (or more) for a deluxe egg salad filling. Chopped green onion may be substituted for regular onion.

For **Egg Salad Wraps**, use tortillas instead of bread slices. Place a layer of lettuce on each tortilla, top with egg salad and wrap; or spread egg salad over tortillas, top with sprouts *or* shredded lettuce, and wrap.

# APPETIZERS, DIPS, SPREADS, AND SAUCES

# Lime and Ginger Mussels

**THESE DELICIOUS TIDBITS** can be prepared early in the day, which takes pressure off the cook around dinner time.

| | |
|---|---|
| 2 lbs. | mussels |
| | brine (p. 126), 1 whole recipe |
| 1 | Roma tomato, diced |
| 1 | medium yellow pepper, diced |
| 2 | green onions, thinly sliced |
| 2 tbsp. | *each*, chopped fresh parsley and dill |
| 3 tbsp. | fresh lime juice |
| 2–3 tbsp. | teriyaki sauce |
| 1 tbsp. | roasted sesame oil |
| 1 tbsp. | minced ginger root |
| | hot pepper sauce, to taste (optional) |
| 1 cup | medium *or* firm tofu, cut into small cubes |
| 1 tbsp. | roasted sesame seeds |

Wash mussels and place them in a large saucepan half-filled with brine. Cover and cook over medium-high heat until mussels open, about 5 minutes. Drain and let cool. Remove mussels from shells, discarding any unopened ones.

In a large bowl, combine mussels, tomato, peppers, onions, parsley, dill, lime juice, teriyaki sauce, oil, ginger and hot pepper sauce, if using. Cover and refrigerate 4 to 6 hours.

About 30 minutes before serving, fold tofu into mussels. Arrange mixture attractively on a bed of mixed greens. Sprinkle with sesame seeds. Serve with garlic bread or toast triangles.

Serves 6 to 8 as an appetizer

PER SERVING: 172 calories, 17 g protein, 13 g carbohydrate, 7 g total fat (1 g saturated fat, 2 g mono, 3 g poly fat), 32 mg cholesterol, 2 g dietary fiber, 333 RE vitamin A, 69 mcg folate, 70 mg vitamin C, 506 mg sodium, 594 mg potassium, 7 mg iron, 98 mg calcium

# Crab-Stuffed Wontons

THESE MAKE DELICIOUS appetizers or wonton soup. Either way, they taste great!

## Stuffing

| | |
|---:|:---|
| 6 oz. | can crabmeat, drained |
| ½ cup | mashed medium tofu |
| 2 tbsp. | crumbled feta cheese |
| 2 tbsp. | mayonnaise |
| 1 | medium celery stalk, finely chopped |
| 2 | green onions, finely chopped |
| 2 tbsp. | roasted sweet red pepper *or* sun-dried tomatoes, finely chopped |
| ¼ tsp. | dried tarragon |
| | pepper, to taste |
| | 30 wonton wraps |

In a medium bowl, combine all stuffing ingredients. Place 1 tsp. of stuffing in the center of each wonton. Brush edges with water. Fold wontons over diagonally to make triangles. Seal edges.

Makes 30 stuffed wontons

## For appetizers you need

| | |
|---:|:---|
| 30 | stuffed wontons |
| ¼ cup | butter, melted |
| 1 tbsp. | sesame seeds |

Preheat oven to 375°F. Sprinkle baking sheet with half of sesame seeds. Brush both sides of stuffed wontons with melted butter. Place on baking sheet and sprinkle with remaining sesame seeds. Bake 10 to 12 minutes, or until stuffed wontons are lightly browned around the edges. Serve warm.

PER WONTON: 59 calories, 2 g protein, 5 g carbohydrate, 3 g total fat (1 g saturated fat, 1 g mono, 1 g poly fat), 12 mg cholesterol, .3 g dietary fiber, 18 RE vitamin A, 3 mcg folate, 1 mg vitamin C, 110 mg sodium, 33 mg potassium, 1 mg iron, 20 mg calcium

## For soup you need

**4 cups**   **chicken or vegetable broth**
**30**   **stuffed wontons**
**2**   **green onions, chopped**

Using a large pot, bring chicken broth to a boil.

Cook stuffed wontons in batches of 6 to 10. Gently drop wontons into boiling broth. Reduce heat to medium-low and let simmer 4 to 5 minutes. Remove cooked wontons with a slotted spoon and set aside. When all wontons are done, return them to the broth and heat through. (A couple of wontons may split open—this is fine as the stuffing will add flavor and texture to the broth.) Just before serving, sprinkle with chopped green onion.

Serves 10

PER SERVING OF SOUP: 145 calories, 9 g protein, 15 g carbohydrate, 5 g total fat (1 g saturated fat, 1 g mono, 2 g poly fat), 24 mg cholesterol, 1 g dietary fiber, 10 RE vitamin A, 12 mcg folate, 3 mg vitamin C, 592 mg sodium, 180 mg potassium, 2 mg iron, 56 mg calcium

**Variations:**

This stuffing can also be used to fill mini tart shells or phyllo pastry; or, easiest of all, it can be spread on baguette slices and broiled 3 to 5 minutes.

# Hot Wonton Crisps

MY FAMILY AND friends always enjoy these spicy and crisp appetizers.

|        |                                                          |
|--------|----------------------------------------------------------|
| 5 oz.  | unripened goat cheese                                    |
| ½ cup  | soft or medium tofu                                      |
| 2 tbsp.| chopped roasted red peppers *or* sun-dried tomatoes      |
|        | generous pinch dried tarragon                            |
|        | salt, to taste                                           |
|        | hot pepper sauce, to taste                               |
| 15     | wonton wraps                                             |
|        | olive oil                                                |
|        | sesame seeds                                             |

In a small bowl, combine goat cheese and tofu with a fork. Mix in roasted peppers, tarragon, salt and hot pepper sauce. Set aside.

Cut each wonton diagonally into 2 triangles. Brush both sides of triangles with olive oil. Place on baking sheet.

Spread each triangle with the goat cheese/tofu mixture. Sprinkle with sesame seeds. (Can be made to this point several hours before serving.)

About 20 minutes before serving, preheat oven to 400°F.

Bake wontons 5 to 7 minutes, or until edges are lightly browned and crisp.

Makes 30 appetizers

PER WONTON CRISP: 27 calories, 1 g protein, 3 g carbohydrate, 1 g total fat (1 g saturated fat, trace mono, trace poly fat), 5 mg cholesterol, .1 g dietary fiber, 7 RE vitamin A, 2 mcg folate, trace vitamin C, 40 mg sodium, 13 mg potassium, .2 mg iron, 9 mg calcium

# Italian Bruschetta

**IF YOU KEEP** garlic butter handy in your refrigerator, this appetizer is a snap to assemble.

> **Italian bread *or* French baguette, sliced**
> **garlic butter (see recipe following)**
> **mozzarella cheese**
> **crumbled firm tofu**
> **finely chopped tomato**
> **chopped chives**
> **salt and pepper**

Spread bread slices generously with garlic butter. Top with mozzarella cheese, tofu, tomato, chives, salt, and pepper. Place bruschetta on a baking sheet and broil in oven until cheese is bubbly and edges of bread slices start to brown. Serve immediately.

# Garlic Butter

I KEEP THIS versatile creamy garlic butter in my refrigerator at all times. It adds flavor to so many dishes and contains only half the butter of regular garlic butter.

| | |
|---:|:---|
| ½ cup | butter, at room temperature |
| ½ cup | grated extra-firm tofu |
| 3 | garlic cloves, minced |
| 1 tbsp. | chopped fresh parsley |
| | salt and pepper, to taste |

Combine all ingredients with a fork until mixture is smooth and creamy. Keeps, refrigerated, for up to 1 week.

Makes just under 1 cup, 1 serving = 1 tbsp.

PER SERVING: 57 calories, trace protein, trace carbohydrate, 6 g total fat (4 g saturated fat, 2 g mono, trace poly fat), 16 mg cholesterol, trace dietary fiber, 58 RE vitamin A, 1 mcg folate, trace vitamin C, 62 mg sodium, 6 mg potassium, trace iron, 4 mg calcium

Garlic butter can be used on bruschetta; for baked or toasted garlic bread; in soups, gravies, or sauces; as a topping for steamed vegetables, pasta, rice, or potatoes; as a seasoning for seafood, meat, poultry, escargots, frogs' legs, and so on.

# Spicy Sun-Dried Tomato Hummus

BE SURE TO have some of this delicious hummus on hand when you have friends over for cocktails. Spread it on crackers or use it as a dip for pita triangles or raw vegetables.

| | |
|---|---|
| 19 oz. | can chickpeas |
| ½ cup | soft or medium tofu |
| 2 tbsp. | tahini |
| 1 | lemon, juice and zest of |
| 2 tbsp. | chopped sun-dried tomatoes, in oil, drained |
| 4 | large garlic cloves, minced |
| 1 tbsp. | chopped fresh dill or basil |
| | soy sauce, to taste |
| | hot pepper sauce, to taste |

In a food processor or blender, process all ingredients until smooth. Cover; refrigerate until ready to use. Keeps several days.

Makes about 2 cups, 1 serving = 1 tsp.

> PER SERVING: 9 calories, trace protein, 1 g carbohydrate, trace total fat (trace saturated fat, trace mono, trace poly fat), 0 mg cholesterol, trace dietary fiber, trace RE vitamin A, 4 mcg folate, 1 mg vitamin C, 18 mg sodium, 14 mg potassium, trace iron, 3 mg calcium

**Variations:**

For **Roasted Red Pepper Hummus**, substitute 2 tbsp. chopped roasted red peppers for sun-dried tomatoes or omit sun-dried tomatoes and soy sauce for a more traditional hummus.

# Avocado Shrimp Bruschetta

A GREAT START to any meal, these appetizers are always a hit.

| | |
|---|---|
| 12 | large cooked shrimp |
| 12 slices | French baguette |

## Marinade

| | |
|---|---|
| 2 | garlic cloves, minced |
| 1 tbsp. | *each*, chopped fresh basil, parsley, chives |
| 1 tbsp. | balsamic vinegar |
| 1 tbsp. | olive oil |
| ¼ cup | diced red pepper |

## Avocado Spread

| | |
|---|---|
| 1 | ripe avocado |
| 3 tbsp. | soft tofu |
| 2 tbsp. | freshly squeezed lemon juice |
| | salt and pepper, to taste |

Place shrimp in a small bowl. Combine marinade ingredients and pour over shrimp. Toss gently. Cover and refrigerate 1 to 3 hours. Toss once or twice before assembling bruschetta.

To make the avocado spread: Combine all ingredients in a blender until smooth. Cover and refrigerate until ready to use (can be made several hours ahead).

Shortly before serving, drain shrimp, herbs and diced pepper. Discard liquid.

Toast or grill baguette slices. Spread generously with avocado spread. Top with shrimp, herbs and peppers. Serve immediately.

Makes 12

PER BRUSCHETTA: 114 calories, 4 g protein, 15 g carbohydrate, 5 g total fat (1 g saturated fat, 3 g mono, 1 g poly fat), 11 mg cholesterol, 2 g dietary fiber, 22 RE vitamin A, 19 mcg folate, 4 mg vitamin C, 167 mg sodium, 140 mg potassium, 1 mg iron, 25 mg calcium

**Variations:**

Instead of shrimp, less expensive "mock" crab is delicious, too. You can use the **Avocado Spread** as a dip for chips or vegetables.

# Salmon Mousse

SERVE THIS DELECTABLE mousse as an appetizer or as a light lunch with a salad or grilled vegetables.

| | |
|---|---|
| 2 x 7.5 oz. | cans salmon |
| 1½ tbsp. | unflavored gelatin (1½ pkgs.) |
| 1 cup | soft *or* medium tofu |
| ½ cup | mayonnaise |
| 1 | lemon, juice of (¼ cup) |
| ½ | medium onion, finely chopped |
| 1 tbsp. | chopped fresh dill *or* cilantro |
| ¼ tsp. | dried tarragon |
| | generous pinch cayenne pepper (optional) |
| | salt and pepper, to taste |

Lightly grease a 4–cup ring mold. Set aside.

Drain salmon, reserving the liquid (about ½ cup). Pour liquid into small saucepan and sprinkle gelatin over it.

In blender or food processor, blend together tofu, mayonnaise and lemon juice until smooth. Add salmon, chopped onion, herbs and seasonings. Process until just combined.

Heat gelatin and salmon liquid over low heat, until gelatin has melted. Stir into salmon mixture. Gently pour into prepared mold. Cover and refrigerate until set, at least 3 hours or overnight.

To unmold mousse, partially fill sink with hot water. Dip bottom of mold into hot water for about 20 seconds. Run a knife around edge of mousse to loosen it. Place a serving platter on top of mold and invert so that mousse slides out. Garnish with sprigs of fresh dill or watercress.

**TO SERVE:** For lunch, serve in slices on small plates on leaf lettuce *or* as an appetizer, serve as a spread with assorted breads and crackers. For a low-calorie variation, serve on cucumber rounds.

Serves 8 to 10 as an appetizer

PER SERVING: 151 calories, 9 g protein, 2 g carbohydrate, 12 g total fat (2 g saturated fat, 1 g mono, 6 g poly fat), 31 mg cholesterol, trace dietary fiber, 8 RE vitamin A, 9 mcg folate, 3 mg vitamin C, 298 mg sodium, 157 mg potassium, .4 mg iron, 95 mg calcium

# Smoked Salmon and Cream Cheese–Tofu Spirals

SMOKED SALMON AND cream cheese are always a winning combination. This lighter version, using half cream cheese and half tofu, is delicious—the dill and capers add extra flavor. Your guests will be delighted with these tasty and pretty appetizers!

| | |
|---|---|
| ½ cup | cream cheese, at room temperature |
| ½ cup | soft tofu |
| 1 tsp. | fresh lemon juice |
| 2 tbsp. | chopped fresh dill |
| 1 tbsp. | capers |
| | salt and pepper, to taste |
| 4 | 10" flour tortillas, preferably pesto green |
| 10 oz. | smoked salmon, thinly sliced |

In a small bowl, combine cream cheese and tofu with a fork until smooth. Mix in lemon juice, dill, capers, salt, and pepper.

Spread each tortilla with the cream cheese/tofu mixture, leaving a 1" border around edge. Arrange salmon in a single layer on top.

Roll up tortillas tightly and wrap in foil or plastic wrap. Refrigerate until ready to serve, 2 hours to overnight.

To serve, trim ends and cut each roll into 8 or 10 slices.

Makes 32 to 40 appetizers

PER SLICE: 31 calories, 2 g protein, 2 g carbohydrate, 2 g total fat (1 g saturated fat, 1 g mono, trace poly fat), 5 mg cholesterol, .1 g dietary fiber, 15 RE vitamin A, 1 mcg folate, trace vitamin C, 89 mg sodium, 21 mg potassium, .2 mg iron, 8 mg calcium

**Variations:**

Use your favorite fresh herbs with or instead of the dill, e.g., chopped parsley, chives or green onions, tarragon, thyme, cilantro, or chervil.

# Roasted Onion
## and Garlic Spread

MY FAMILY AND I enjoy this flavorful spread so much that we sometimes make a meal of it. Just add a salad and a glass of wine!

|   |   |
|---|---|
| 2 | large sweet onions, coarsely chopped |
| 10 | medium garlic cloves, quartered |
| 2 tbsp. | olive oil |
| 1 tbsp. | honey |
| ⅓ cup | soft tofu |
|   | salt and pepper, to taste |

Preheat oven to 350°F. Combine first 4 ingredients in a baking dish. Bake, uncovered, 1½ to 2 hours; stir occasionally to prevent browning. Transfer to food processor with the tofu, salt and pepper. Process until almost smooth or leave slightly chunky. Serve warm on toasted baguette slices. Leftover spread can be reheated or used to season other dishes.

Makes about 1 cup, 1 serving = 1 tsp.

PER SERVING: 10 calories, trace protein, 1 g carbohydrate, 1 g total fat (trace saturated fat, trace mono, trace poly fat), 0 mg cholesterol, trace dietary fiber, 0 RE vitamin A, 1 mcg folate, 1 mg vitamin C, trace sodium, 13 mg potassium, trace iron, 3 mg calcium

# Aïoli-Garlic Mayonnaise

IN PROVENCE THIS garlicky mayonnaise is used as a rich-tasting butter substitute. Serve with hot or cold fish or on vegetables and eggs. For a delicious garnish, spread on toasted baguette slices and float on hot or cold soups.

|        |                         |
|-------:|-------------------------|
| 1      | egg yolk                |
| 1 tbsp. | Dijon mustard          |
| 2 tbsp. | soft tofu              |
| 1–2    | garlic cloves, crushed  |
| ½ cup  | olive oil               |
|        | pepper, to taste        |
|        | few drops of lemon juice |

In a small bowl, blend together egg yolk, mustard, tofu, and garlic until smooth. Gradually add the oil, drop by drop, whisking constantly until mayonnaise is thick. Whisk in pepper and lemon juice. Cover and chill. Keeps several days, refrigerated.

Makes 2/3 cup, 1 serving = 1 tsp.

PER SERVING: 33 calories, trace protein, trace carbohydrate, 4 g total fat (1 g saturated fat, 3 g mono, trace poly fat), 7 mg cholesterol, trace dietary fiber, 3 RE vitamin A, 1 mcg folate, trace vitamin C, 3 mg sodium, 2 mg potassium, trace iron, 2 mg calcium

**Variations:**

To make **Skordalia** or **Potato Garlic Mayonnaise**, a lighter Greek variation, whisk in ½ cup of warm mashed potatoes.

# Creamy Blue Cheese Spread

GREAT AS AN appetizer with crackers or after dinner with a glass of port.

| | |
|---|---|
| 8 oz. | blue cheese, at room temperature |
| I cup | medium tofu |
| ¼ cup | cream cheese, at room temperature |
| I–2 tbsp. | brandy |
| | generous pinch dried tarragon |
| | pepper, to taste |

Combine all ingredients in a food processor until smooth. Cover and refrigerate until ready to serve. Keeps several days, refrigerated.

Makes about 2 cups, 1 serving = 1 tbsp.

PER SERVING: 38 calories, 2 g protein, trace carbohydrate, 3 g total fat (2 g saturated fat, I g mono, trace poly fat), 7 mg cholesterol, trace dietary fiber, 25 RE vitamin A, 4 mcg folate, trace vitamin C, 105 mg sodium, 30 mg potassium, trace iron, 47 mg calcium

# Taramasalata

MY NEIGHBOR Mina Kotsopoulos introduced me to this flavorful Greek appetizer. Adding tofu reduces the olive oil in the traditional recipe by more than half. Pale orange carp roe caviar (tarama) is available in large supermarkets or Greek grocery stores.

| | |
|---:|:---|
| I lb. | potatoes (3 *or* 4 medium) |
| ¼ cup | carp roe caviar, or to taste |
| ¼ cup | olive oil |
| ½ cup | soft *or* medium tofu |
| 2 | lemons, juice of |
| 2 | garlic cloves, minced (optional) |

Cook potatoes in boiling water until tender. Drain and peel. In a food processor, process all ingredients until smooth. Adjust seasonings. Serve warm or at room temperature on a bed of greens with your favorite bread, crackers or as a dip for raw vegetables.

Makes about 3 cups, 1 serving = 1 tbsp.

PER SERVING: 21 calories, 1 g protein, 2 g carbohydrate, 1 g total fat (trace saturated fat, 1 g mono, trace poly fat), 4 mg cholesterol, trace dietary fiber, 1 RE vitamin A, 2 mcg folate, 3 mg vitamin C, 2 mg sodium, 42 mg potassium, trace iron, 1 mg calcium

# Honey Garlic Peanut Sauce

A GREAT DIPPING sauce for shrimp or scallops, or spoon it over poached or grilled seafood.

| | |
|---|---|
| ¼ cup | soft tofu |
| 1 | orange, juice of |
| ½ | lemon, juice of |
| ¼ cup | smooth peanut butter |
| 2 tbsp. | honey |
| 2 | garlic cloves, minced |
| ¼ cup | chopped fresh basil |
| 1 tbsp. | minced ginger root |
| 1–2 tbsp. | soy sauce |
| | pepper, to taste |

In a small saucepan, with an electric hand blender, blend together tofu, orange and lemon juice until smooth. Add remaining ingredients, cover, and simmer over low heat, about 5 minutes. Serve immediately or refrigerate up to 3 days. Heat just before serving. If sauce is too thick, stir in a little water and adjust seasonings.

Makes about 1 cup, 1 serving = 1 tbsp.

PER SERVING: 36 calories, 1 g protein, 4g carbohydrate, 2 g total fat (trace saturated fat, 1 g mono, 1 g poly fat), 0 mg cholesterol, .2 g dietary fiber, 3 RE vitamin A, 5 mcg folate, 3 mg vitamin C, 84 mg sodium, 48 mg potassium, .1 mg iron, 5 mg calcium

# Béchamel Sauce
# with Cheese

**WITHOUT THE CHEESE,** this versatile, rich-tasting sauce is the basis for many dishes: cream soups, casseroles, gravies, etc. With the cheese, serve over cooked vegetables, fish, eggs, crêpes, pasta, etc. You'll love its creamy texture, even though this version is made without cream or added fat!

| | |
|---|---|
| I cup | milk |
| I cup | soft tofu |
| ½–I | bouillon cube, vegetable, chicken *or* beef, crumbled |
| ¼ cup | unbleached flour |
| ½ cup | grated Cheddar *or* Swiss cheese |
| | salt and pepper to taste |

In a medium saucepan, with an electric hand blender, blend together milk, tofu, bouillon cube and flour until smooth. Over medium-high heat, whisk until mixture comes to a boil. Reduce heat to low, whisking vigorously to prevent lumping or to smooth out any lumps that may have formed. When sauce is smooth, fold in cheese and seasonings. Cook and stir another 2 minutes, until cheese has melted. If sauce is too thick, add a little milk or water; if it is too runny, let it simmer a few more minutes, uncovered, until the desired consistency is reached.

Makes about 2 cups, serves 6, 1 serving = ⅓ cup

> PER SERVING: 53 calories, 3 g protein, 7 g carbohydrate, I g total fat (trace saturated fat, trace mono, trace poly fat), 3 mg cholesterol, 0 g dietary fiber, 23 RE vitamin A, 2 mcg folate, trace vitamin C, 188 mg sodium, 68 mg potassium, .4 mg iron, 54 mg calcium

> ORIGINAL RECIPE PER SERVING: 140 calories, 3 g protein, 8 g carbohydrate, I I g total fat (2 g saturated fat, 4 g mono, 4 g poly fat), 6 mg cholesterol, 0 g dietary fiber, 53 RE vitamin A, 4 mcg folate, I g vitamin C, 41 mg sodium, 131 mg potassium, .3 mg iron, 106 mg calcium

**Variations:**

Traditional Béchamel Sauce has no cheese and the milk is simmered with a small onion, bay leaf, whole clove, and a pinch of nutmeg. Other variations are: **Mornay**, with grated Cheddar or Swiss cheese *or* Parmesan and Gruyère *or* blue, Roquefort, Stilton or Gorgonzola, to taste. **Mustard Sauce**, with 2 to 3 tbsp. smooth or grainy Dijon or English mustard added. **Curry Sauce**, with 1 large chopped onion, 1 to 2 tsp. curry powder sautéed in 1 to 2 tbsp. butter added to basic Béchamel, without cheese or bouillon.

# Tartar Sauce

SERVE THIS LIGHTER version with fish or vegetables.

| | |
|---|---|
| ½ cup | soft tofu |
| 2 tbsp. | mayonnaise |
| 2 tbsp. | plain yogurt |
| 2 tbsp. | sweet pickle relish |
| | salt and pepper, to taste |

In a small bowl, whisk together tofu, mayonnaise, and yogurt. Fold in relish, salt, and pepper. Cover; refrigerate until ready to serve.

Makes just under 1 cup, 1 serving = 1 tbsp.

PER SERVING: 18 calories, trace protein, I g carbohydrate, 2 g total fat (trace saturated fat, trace mono, I g poly fat), I mg cholesterol, trace dietary fiber, I RE vitamin A, trace folate, trace vitamin C, 26 mg sodium, 5 mg potassium, trace iron, 4 mg calcium

# SOUPS
### AND SALADS

# Miniature Dumpling Soup

TO MAKE THIS delicious soup from scratch takes about 5 minutes longer than to heat up a can of soup. And of course it's *much* better for you than any canned soup! It calls for lovage, a perennial herb that has a strong celerylike flavor. Substitute celery leaves or feel free to use oregano, parsley, basil, thyme, marjoram, summer savory, rosemary, and so on.

| | |
|---:|:---|
| 2 | eggs |
| ¼ cup | soft tofu |
| ¼ cup | unbleached flour |
| pinch | salt |
| 4 cups | chicken *or* vegetable broth |
| 1–2 tbsp. | chopped fresh lovage *or* other herbs |
| ½ cup | cubed medium *or* firm tofu |
| 1 tsp. | chopped fresh chives, for garnish |

In a small bowl, with a hand blender, blend together eggs and soft tofu. Fold in flour and salt. Set aside.

In a medium saucepan, bring broth and herbs to a boil. Slowly drop small spoonfuls of batter into boiling broth, stirring gently, until little dumplings rise to the surface, about 1 minute. Stir in cubed tofu. Heat through and serve garnished with chives.

Serves 4 to 6

PER SERVING: 89 calories, 8 g protein, 5 g carbohydrate, 4 g total fat (1 g saturated fat, 1 g mono, 1 g poly fat), 71 mg cholesterol, .3 g dietary fiber, 36 RE vitamin A, 15 mcg folate, trace vitamin C, 540 mg sodium, 193 mg potassium, 2 mg iron, 38 mg calcium

# Leek and Potato Soup

EASY TO MAKE, healthy and satisfying, this delicious low-fat soup is a great start to any meal.

|  |  |
|---|---|
| 2½ cups | chicken, beef or vegetable broth, divided |
| 2 | large leeks, white and light green parts only, chopped |
| 2 | large potatoes, peeled, diced |
| 1 tbsp. | chopped fresh parsley *or* cilantro *or* 1 tsp. dried |
| ½ cup | soft *or* medium tofu |
| ½ cup | cubed firm tofu (optional) |
|  | salt and pepper, to taste |
| 1 tbsp. | chopped fresh chives, for garnish |

In a large saucepan, over high heat, bring 2 cups of chicken broth to a boil. Add leeks, potatoes and parsley. Reduce heat to low, cover and let simmer 20 to 25 minutes, or until vegetables are soft.

Using a food processor or blender, purée vegetable mixture with soft tofu until smooth. Return soup to saucepan. If soup is too thick, add remaining ½ cup broth. Fold in cubed tofu, if using. Heat through and adjust seasonings. To serve, garnish with chives.

Serves 4

PER SERVING: 130 calories, 6 g protein, 23 g carbohydrate, 2 g total fat (trace saturated fat, trace mono, 1 g poly fat), 0 mg cholesterol, 2 g dietary fiber, 14 RE vitamin A, 52 mcg folate, 18 mg vitamin C, 502 mg sodium, 508 mg potassium, 2 mg iron, 52 mg calcium

# Winter Vegetable Soup

IF YOU HAVE a food processor or an electric chopper to chop the vegetables, this flavorful and rich-textured, almost fat-free soup is a snap to prepare. And, oh, so deliciously healthy! Serve it with garlic bread or bruschetta.

| | |
|---|---|
| 4 cups | chicken or vegetable broth |
| 2 | large leeks, white and light green parts only, chopped |
| 3 cups | peeled, diced squash |
| 2 cups | diced carrots |
| 1 | medium onion, chopped |
| 1 | large potato, peeled, chopped |
| 1 | medium apple, peeled, chopped |
| 2 | medium celery stalks, chopped |
| 1 | garlic clove, minced |
| 1 tbsp. | chopped fresh tarragon or 1 tsp. dried |
| 1 cup | soft or medium tofu |
| | salt and pepper, to taste |
| ¼ cup | diced medium or firm tofu for garnish |
| 2 tbsp. | chopped fresh chives for garnish |

In a large saucepan, over high heat, bring chicken broth to a boil. Add vegetables, apple, garlic, and tarragon. Return to a boil. Reduce heat to low; cover and let simmer 20 to 25 minutes, or until vegetables are soft.

Using a food processor or blender, purée vegetable mixture with soft tofu, until smooth. Return soup to saucepan. Adjust seasonings. Heat through. To serve, garnish with diced tofu and chives.

Serves 4 to 6

PER SERVING: 165 calories, 8 g protein, 30 g carbohydrate, 3 g total fat (trace saturated fat, 1 g mono, 1 g poly fat), 0 mg cholesterol, 5 g dietary fiber, 2231 RE vitamin A, 65 mcg folate, 25 mg vitamin C, 568 mg sodium, 847 mg potassium, 3 mg iron, 98 mg calcium

# Seafood Chowder

THIS NUTRITIOUS LOW-FAT soup can be a meal by itself. Serve it with **Multigrain Health Bread** (p. 30).

| | |
|---|---|
| 1 cup | fish stock *or* chicken *or* vegetable broth |
| 1 | large carrot, diced |
| 1 | large celery stalk, diced |
| 1 | large potato, diced |
| 2 | green onions, thinly sliced |
| 2 | garlic cloves, minced |
| 1 tbsp. | *each*, chopped fresh parsley and dill |
| 1 cup | soft tofu |
| 2 cups | milk |
| 1 cup | dry white wine |
| 3 tbsp. | unbleached flour |
| 1 | bouillon cube *or* soy sauce, to taste |
| ½ lb. | fish fillets (cod, haddock, salmon, *or* ocean perch), in bite-sized pieces |
| 4 oz. | can cooked medium shrimp, drained and rinsed |
| 5 oz. | can cooked clams, including juice |
| ½–¾ cup | cubed medium tofu |
| 3 tbsp. | whipping cream (optional) |
| | salt and pepper, to taste |
| | sprigs of dill, for garnish |

In a medium saucepan, bring broth to a boil. Add vegetables, garlic, parsley, and dill. Cover. Reduce heat to low; simmer 10 to 15 minutes, until vegetables are tender. Remove from heat.

In a large saucepan, blend together soft tofu, milk, wine, and flour with hand blender. Bring to a boil. When thickened, add vegetables, broth, and bouillon. Fold in fish; reduce heat to low; simmer 2 to 3 minutes, until fish is just tender. Add shrimp, clams with juice, cubed tofu and cream, if using. Mix gently; heat through. Adjust seasonings. Garnish with dill sprigs.

Serves 6

PER SERVING: 205 calories, 18 g protein, 19 g carbohydrate, 3 g total fat (1 g saturated fat, 1 g mono, 1 g poly fat), 45 mg cholesterol, 2 g dietary fiber, 402 RE vitamin A, 25 mcg folate, 14 mg vitamin C, 451 mg sodium, 777 mg potassium, 3 mg iron, 166 mg calcium

# Cream of Spinach Soup

THIS RICH-TASTING cream soup (without the cream!) is always a favorite, especially on cold winter days.

|  |  |
|---|---|
|  | **Creamed Spinach (p. 86), 1 whole recipe** |
| 1½–2 cups | **chicken or vegetable broth** |
| 2 tbsp. | **chopped fresh herbs** |
|  | **salt and pepper, to taste** |

Make creamed spinach.

Over medium heat, slowly stir broth into creamed spinach until desired consistency is reached. Stir in herbs, salt and pepper. Bring to a boil and serve.

Serves 4 to 6

PER SERVING: 89 calories, 7 g protein, 12 g carbohydrate, 2 g total fat (1 g saturated fat, 1 g mono, 1 g poly fat), 3 mg cholesterol, 3 g dietary fiber, 758 RE vitamin A, 105 mcg folate, 12 mg vitamin C, 783 mg sodium, 403 mg potassium, 2 mg iron, 195 mg calcium

**Variations:**

Try this recipe with creamed Swiss chard, broccoli, or leeks; just substitute them for the spinach in the **Creamed Spinach** recipe.

# Asparagus Salad

THE PRESENTATION OF this multicolored salad makes it ideal for a festive occasion.

| | |
|---:|:---|
| 24 | asparagus spears, woody ends removed |
| 1 | yellow *or* orange pepper, julienned |
| 2 | ripe medium-sized tomatoes, sliced |
| 1 | small red onion, thinly sliced |
| 1 cup | cubed medium *or* firm tofu |
| ¾ cup | All-Purpose Salad Dressing (p. 80) |

Heat a large saucepan half-filled with water. When water boils, gently add asparagus. Reduce heat to medium and continue cooking, uncovered, 7 to 10 minutes, or until asparagus spears are tender crisp. Remove from heat and drain well.

Stack asparagus in the center of a large, oval platter. Attractively arrange peppers and tomatoes around the asparagus. Top asparagus with onions and tofu. While still warm, spoon **All-Purpose Salad Dressing** over entire salad. Cool to room temperature. Cover and refrigerate until ready to serve.

Serves 4 to 6

PER SERVING: 163 calories, 6 g protein, 11 g carbohydrate, 12 g total fat (2 g saturated fat, 7 g mono, 2 g poly fat), 0 mg cholesterol, 2 g dietary fiber, 89 RE vitamin A, 105 mcg folate, 82 mg vitamin C, 109 mg sodium, 372 mg potassium, 3 mg iron, 70 mg calcium

# Salad Combinations
# Using Tofu

ADD FIRM TOFU—cubed, julienned, crumbled or grated—as well as chopped fresh herbs to any of the following salad combinations:

- mixed greens
  chopped tomato
  sliced sweet onion
  sliced mushroom
- lettuce
  grated carrot
  sliced apple
  sliced sweet onion
  pecan *or* walnut halves
  raisins
- cooked chickpeas
  sliced green onion
  chopped tomato
  crumbled feta
  broccoli florets
  pine nuts, sunflower seeds *or* toasted almonds
  crumbled bacon
- cooked lentils
  chopped onion
  chopped tomato
  chopped green pepper
- cooked kidney beans
  cooked corn kernels
  sliced green onion
  chopped roasted red pepper
- cooked white beans
  diced sun-dried tomatoes

- chopped green pepper
- sliced green onion
- ◼ sliced tomato
- sliced olives
- chopped onion
- crumbled feta *or* goat cheese
- ◼ Belgian endives
- chopped ham
- walnut *or* pecan halves
- cubed Cheddar
- ◼ raw spinach leaves
- sliced apple
- cubed Brie, at room temperature
- pine nuts
- ◼ cooked green beans
- sliced red onion
- crumbled bacon
- ◼ chopped cucumber
- shrimp, crab *or* mock crab
- sliced green onion

Toss each of the above salads with the **All-Purpose Salad Dressing** (p. 80)

# All-Purpose Salad Dressing

THIS DRESSING IS suitable for every type of salad—tomato, pasta, bean, carrot, tossed greens, etc.

| | |
|---|---|
| ½ cup | **soft or medium tofu** |
| 3 tbsp. | **balsamic vinegar** |
| ¼ cup | **olive oil** |
| 1–2 | **large garlic cloves, minced** |
| 1 tbsp. | **chopped fresh parsley** |
| ¼ tsp. | **salt, or to taste** |
| | **generous pinch of pepper** |

In a food processor or with an electric hand blender, blend together tofu, vinegar, and oil. Fold in garlic, parsley, salt, and pepper. Cover and refrigerate until ready to use, up to 2 days. If oil separates, whisk dressing before serving.

Makes ¾ cup, 1 serving = 1 tbsp.

PER SERVING: 47 calories, trace protein, 1 g carbohydrate, 5 g total fat (1 g saturated fat, 3 g mono, trace poly fat), 0 mg cholesterol, trace dietary fiber, 2 RE vitamin A, trace folate, 1 mg vitamin C, 50 mg sodium, 7 mg potassium, .2 mg iron, 2 mg calcium

**Variations:**
1. Instead of parsley, try basil, tarragon or cilantro.
2. For a nippier dressing, add crushed chili peppers and a little crumbled feta, goat or blue cheese.
3. For a more mellow dressing, add a little honey or sugar.
4. For extra flavor, add capers or chopped olives.

# Pasta Salad

THIS NUTRITIOUS AND tasty pasta salad can be part of an elegant dinner or a casual brunch.

| | |
|---|---|
| ¾ cup | **All-Purpose Salad Dressing (p. 80)** |
| 1½ cups | **uncooked rotini** |
| 1½ cups | **raw asparagus tips, cut 2" long** |
| 6 | **cherry tomatoes, halved** |
| ½ cup | **roasted sweet red peppers, cut into thin strips** |
| 6 | **fresh basil leaves, shredded** |
| 2 | **green onions, thinly sliced** |
| 2 tbsp. | **sliced olives** |
| 2 tbsp. | **pine nuts** |
| ¾ cup | **extra-firm tofu, cut into cubes *or* strips** |
| 1 tbsp. | **crumbled feta cheese** |

Make salad dressing. Set aside.

Bring a large pot of water to a boil. Add rotini. Simmer 5 minutes. Add asparagus and simmer another 5 minutes, or until rotini and asparagus are just tender. Drain.

Transfer rotini and asparagus to a large bowl. Add remaining ingredients.

Pour ½ of dressing over pasta mixture. Toss gently. Add more dressing, if desired. Cover and refrigerate.

Just before serving, adjust seasonings and toss salad once more.

Serves 6 to 8

PER SERVING: 172 calories, 7 g protein, 12 g carbohydrate, 12 g total fat (2 g saturated fat, 7 g mono, 3 g poly fat), 2 mg cholesterol, 2 g dietary fiber, 78 RE vitamin A, 60 mcg folate, 27 mg vitamin C, 172 mg sodium, 219 mg potassium, 4 mg iron, 75 mg calcium

# VEGETABLES
### AND SIDE DISHES

# Bok Choy and Pears in Honey Ginger Sauce

THIS MILDLY SWEET-AND-SOUR combination of vegetables, pears, tofu and nuts makes for a healthy low-fat dish.

### Honey Ginger Sauce

| | |
|---|---|
| 1 tbsp. | tahini or peanut butter |
| 1 tbsp. | honey |
| 2–3 tbsp. | teriyaki sauce |
| | generous pinch red pepper flakes |
| ½ | lemon, juice of |
| 1 cup | cubed firm tofu |
| 1 tbsp. | roasted sesame oil |
| 1 lb. | bok choy, cut into bite-sized pieces |
| 1 | large carrot, julienned |
| 1 tbsp. | diced ginger root |
| ¼ cup | dried pears, julienned |
| 2 tbsp. | whole almonds |
| 1 tbsp. | toasted sesame seeds |

In a small saucepan, combine sauce ingredients. Over low heat, stir sauce until smooth. Remove from heat.

Fold tofu into sauce. Set aside.

In a wok or other deep nonstick frying pan, heat oil. Over high heat, stir-fry bok choy, carrots, and ginger root for 2 to 3 minutes. Add pears, almonds, tofu, and sauce. Reduce heat to medium and stir-fry another 1 to 2 minutes, until heated through. Adjust seasonings.

Just before serving, sprinkle with sesame seeds.

Serves 4 to 6

PER SERVING: 168 calories, 10 g protein, 15 g carbohydrate, 9 g total fat (1 g saturated fat, 3 g mono, 4 g poly fat), 0 mg cholesterol, 3 g dietary fiber, 460 RE vitamin A, 69 mcg folate, 50 mg vitamin C, 283 mg sodium, 399 mg potassium, 6 mg iron, 180 mg calcium

# Creamed Spinach

FEW PEOPLE LIKE plain spinach. Most cooks dress it up with lots of fattening cream—not necessary when you try the following creamy yet low-fat recipe.

| | |
|---|---|
| **2 cups** | **Béchamel Sauce (p. 66), 1 recipe** |
| **2 x 10 oz.** | **packages fresh *or* frozen spinach** |
| | **salt and pepper to taste** |

Make a thick **Béchamel Sauce**. Cover and set aside.

Cook spinach according to package directions. If using fresh, cook in ½ cup boiling water for 5 minutes. Pour into sieve to drain. Squeeze out excess water. Chop spinach in food processor. Fold into Béchamel Sauce. Cook over low heat; stir until it begins to bubble. Adjust seasonings.

Serves 4 to 6

PER SERVING: 79 calories, 6 g protein, 12 g carbohydrate, 2 g total fat (1 g saturated fat, trace mono, trace poly fat), 3 mg cholesterol, 3 g dietary fiber, 758 RE vitamin A, 104 mcg folate, 12 mg vitamin C, 269 mg sodium, 350 mg potassium, 2 mg iron, 192 mg calcium

**Variations:**

Try this recipe with Swiss chard, broccoli, or leeks.

# Spinach Soufflè

THIS LIGHT AND elegant dish takes just a few minutes longer to prepare than **Creamed Spinach**; however, it requires an hour of baking.

**Creamed Spinach (p. 86), 1 whole recipe**
**2   eggs, separated**

Make creamed spinach. Do not add any extra liquid as it should be very
thick. Mix in egg yolks. Beat egg whites until stiff and gently fold into the
creamed spinach. Pour into a greased 8" baking dish. Bake at 350°F about 1
hour, or until puffy and lightly browned. Serve immediately.

Serves 6

PER SERVING: 104 calories, 8 g protein, 12 g carbohydrate, 3 g total fat (1 g saturated fat, 1 g mono, 1 g poly fat), 74 mg cholesterol, 3 g dietary fiber, 790 RE vitamin A, 111 mcg folate, 12 mg vitamin C, 290 mg sodium, 370 mg potassium, 2 mg
iron, 200 mg calcium

**Variations:**
Try this recipe with creamed Swiss chard or leeks.

# Zesty Zucchini

| | |
|---|---|
| 1 tbsp. | vegetable oil |
| ½–1 cup | cubed firm tofu |
| | salt and pepper, to taste |
| 3 | medium zucchini, cut into bite-sized pieces |
| 1 | medium ripe tomato, diced |
| 1 | small onion, chopped |
| 1 | garlic clove, minced |
| 1 tbsp. | chopped fresh cilantro |
| | soy sauce, to taste |
| | hot pepper sauce, to taste |

Heat oil in a medium saucepan. Add tofu, salt, and pepper and, over high heat, sauté until golden. Remove tofu and set aside. Add remaining ingredients to saucepan. Bring to a boil and reduce heat to medium. Cook, uncovered, 10 to 15 minutes, or until zucchini is just tender. Adjust seasonings. Fold in tofu, heat through and serve.

Serves 4

PER SERVING: 98 calories, 6 g protein, 6 g carbohydrate, 7 g total fat (1 g saturated fat, 2 g mono, 3 g poly fat), 0 mg cholesterol, 2 g dietary fiber, 45 RE vitamin A, 24 mcg folate, 19 mg vitamin C, 9 mg sodium, 333 mg potassium, 4 mg iron, 82 mg calcium

# Spanish Eggplant

| | |
|---|---|
| 1 | large *or* 2 medium ripe tomatoes, diced |
| 1–2 | garlic cloves, minced |
| 1 tbsp. | *each*, chopped fresh basil, parsley, lovage (or other favorite herbs) |
| 1 tsp. | olive oil |
| | salt and pepper, to taste |
| 1 | large eggplant, ends removed, sliced into 6 to 8 rounds |
| ½ cup | grated Cheddar cheese |
| ½ cup | coarsely chopped medium tofu |
| ½ cup | shredded mozzarella cheese |

In a small bowl, combine tomato, garlic, herbs, olive oil, salt, and pepper. Set aside.

Arrange eggplant slices in a single layer in a lightly greased baking dish. Sprinkle with salt and pepper. Spread Cheddar, then tofu, evenly over rounds. Top with tomato mixture and mozzarella. Bake at 400°F about 15 minutes, or until eggplant is soft and cheese is bubbly.

Serves 2 as a main dish or 6 as a side dish

PER SIDE DISH SERVING: 119 calories, 8 g protein, 8 g carbohydrate, 7 g total fat (3 g saturated fat, 2 g mono, 1 g poly fat), 15 mg cholesterol, 3 g dietary fiber, 102 RE vitamin A, 29 mcg folate, 11 mg vitamin C, 116 mg sodium, 309 mg potassium, 2 mg iron, 178 mg calcium

# Baked Onions with Stewed Tomatoes

THE AROMA OF this dish makes your mouth water. Very little fat, great flavor!

| | |
|---|---|
| 6 | medium cooking onions, peeled and cut in half crosswise |
| ½ cup | coarsely chopped medium tofu |
| 2 tbsp. | coarsely chopped sun-dried tomatoes |
| | salt and pepper, to taste |
| 14 fl. oz. | can stewed tomatoes |
| ¼ cup | shredded mozzarella cheese |

Arrange onions, cut side up, in a shallow, lightly greased baking dish. Spread tofu and sun-dried tomatoes over onions. Sprinkle with salt and pepper. Spoon stewed tomatoes over onions. Cover lightly with aluminum foil. Bake at 350°F for 30 minutes.

Remove foil and bake another 30 to 40 minutes, or until onions are soft. Top with mozzarella cheese and return to oven 5 minutes longer, until cheese has melted.

Serves 4 to 6

PER SERVING: 103 calories, 5 g protein, 17 g carbohydrate, 3 g total fat (1 g saturated fat, 1 g mono, 1 g poly fat), 3 mg cholesterol, 3 g dietary fiber, 66 RE vitamin A, 26 mcg folate, 15 mg vitamin C, 182 mg sodium, 249 mg potassium, 2 mg iron, 103 mg calcium

# Mushroom and Tofu Medley

| ½ lb. | mushrooms (e.g., a combination of crimini, oyster, and button mushrooms) |
| 1 tbsp. | vegetable oil |
| 1 tbsp. | butter |
| 1 | small onion, thinly sliced |
| ½–1 cup | cubed firm *or* extra-firm tofu |
| 2 tbsp. | chopped fresh cilantro |
| | generous pinch dried oregano |
| | salt and pepper, to taste |

Wash mushrooms and cut in half or into large pieces.

In a deep, nonstick frying pan, heat oil and butter. Add onions, mushrooms, and tofu, and sauté over medium-high heat about 5 minutes, or until lightly browned. Add cilantro, oregano, salt, and pepper. Sauté another 1 to 2 minutes. Serve immediately or cover and reheat when ready to serve.

Serves 4 to 6

PER SERVING: 95 calories, 7 g protein, 6 g carbohydrate, 6 g total fat (2 g saturated fat, 1 g mono, 2 g poly fat), 8 mg cholesterol, 2 g dietary fiber, 41 RE vitamin A, 25 mcg folate, 4 mg vitamin C, 40 mg sodium, 329 mg potassium, 4 mg iron, 76 mg calcium

# Gingered Carrots

PLAIN STEAMED CARROTS can be quite bland. The ginger, corn relish and tofu in this recipe give the carrots a little pizzazz. Try it!

| | |
|---|---|
| 1 tbsp. | vegetable oil |
| 1 lb. | carrots, thinly sliced crosswise |
| 1 | green onion, thinly sliced |
| 1 tbsp. | minced ginger root |
| 1 tsp. | sugar |
| | salt to taste |
| ¼ cup | water |
| ¼ cup | sweet whole kernel corn relish |
| ½–1 cup | firm *or* extra-firm tofu, cut into small cubes |

In a medium saucepan over high heat, heat oil. Add carrots, onion, ginger, sugar, and salt, and sauté 1 minute. Add water and cover. Reduce heat to low and let simmer about 10 minutes, or until carrots are tender crisp.

Add corn relish and tofu. Increase heat to medium-high and continue cooking, uncovered, about 5 minutes, or until most of the liquid has evaporated.

Serves 4 to 6

PER SERVING: 100 calories, 4 g protein, 13 g carbohydrate, 4 g total fat (1 g saturated fat, 1 g mono, 2 g poly fat), 0 mg cholesterol, 3 g dietary fiber, 2133 RE vitamin A, 18 mcg folate, 8 mg vitamin C, 111 mg sodium, 304 mg potassium, 3 mg iron, 67 mg calcium

# Mashed Parsnips

THESE MAKE A delicious alternative to mashed potatoes.

| | |
|---|---|
| ½ cup | water |
| 1 lb. | parsnips, cleaned, sliced |
| | salt and pepper, to taste |
| ½ cup | soft tofu |
| 2 tbsp. | maple syrup |
| 1 tbsp. | butter (optional) |

Bring water to a boil in a medium saucepan. Add parsnips, salt, and pepper. Return to a boil, then reduce heat to low, cover and let simmer about 20 minutes, stirring occasionally. If all liquid is absorbed, add a little water.

When parsnips are tender, remove from heat. Using a hand blender, mix tofu, maple syrup, and butter, if using, into parsnips. Mashed parsnips should have the consistency of mashed potatoes.

Serves 3 to 4

PER SERVING: 124 calories, 2 g protein, 29 g carbohydrate, 1 g total fat (trace saturated fat, trace mono, trace poly fat), 0 mg cholesterol, 5 g dietary fiber, 0 RE vitamin A, 66 mcg folate, 15 mg vitamin C, 14 mg sodium, 433 mg potassium, 1 mg iron, 56 mg calcium

**Variations:**

Try squash, sweet potatoes, or turnips instead of parsnips.

# Cauliflower with Light Cheese Sauce

LIGHT YET NUTRITIOUS, this tasty dish goes well with pasta, couscous, or potatoes.

| | |
|---:|:---|
| 1 | medium cauliflower, about 2 lbs. |
| 3 cups | water |
| ½ cup | unbleached flour |
| ½ cup | soft *or* medium tofu |
| 1 | vegetable *or* chicken bouillon cube |
| 1 cup | grated Cheddar *or* Swiss cheese, divided |
| ½–1 cup | cubed firm tofu |
| 2 tbsp. | bread crumbs |
| 1 tbsp. | butter (optional) |

Break cauliflower into florets and rinse thoroughly. In a large saucepan, bring water to a boil. Add cauliflower; cover and reduce heat to low. Simmer 5 to 7 minutes, or until cauliflower is tender crisp. Drain; reserve 2 cups of the cooking water.

In a medium saucepan, blend together the soft tofu and cooking water with a whisk. Whisk flour in quickly to prevent lumping. Over medium heat, bring to a boil, whisking constantly. When thickened, reduce heat to low. Stir in bouillon cube and ¾ cup of cheese.

Spread cauliflower florets in a baking dish and sprinkle with tofu cubes. Pour cheese sauce over them. Top with remaining cheese and bread crumbs. Dot with butter, if desired.

Broil in top rack of oven for about 5 minutes, or until cheese sauce is bubbly and starting to brown. Turn off heat; close oven door and let sit 5 to 10 minutes longer before serving.

Serves 4 to 6

PER SERVING: 187 calories, 13 g protein, 15 g carbohydrate, 9 g total fat (4 g saturated fat, 2 g mono, 2 g poly fat), 20 mg cholesterol, 4 g dietary fiber, 63 RE vitamin
A, 10 mcg folate, 99 mg vitamin C, 358 mg sodium, 522 mg potassium, 4 mg iron,
220 mg calcium

**Variations:**

For a slightly richer sauce, substitute 1 cup milk for 1 cup cooking
water. Broccoli, peas, and corn also taste great with cheese sauce.

# Garlic Mashed Potatoes

THIS ULTRA-LIGHT version of mashed potatoes is nutritious and delicious with the added flavor of garlic and herbs. Since mashed potatoes are usually served with gravy, it is unnecessary to add extra fat (milk and butter) to them.

|        |                                      |
|-------:|--------------------------------------|
| 4      | large potatoes, such as Yukon Gold   |
| 1 cup  | potato cooking water                 |
| 4–6    | garlic cloves, peeled, halved        |
| ¾ cup  | soft *or* medium tofu                |
|        | salt and pepper, to taste            |
| 2 tbsp.| chopped fresh cilantro *or* basil    |
| 1 tbsp.| butter (optional)                    |

Peel and quarter potatoes. Half fill a large saucepan with water. Bring water to a boil and add potatoes and garlic. Cover. Reduce heat to medium low and simmer until potatoes and garlic are tender, 15 to 20 minutes. Drain, reserving 1 cup of the cooking water.

In a large bowl, mash potatoes and garlic.

In a small bowl, with a hand blender, blend together the tofu and ½ cup of the reserved cooking water. Gradually add to the mashed potatoes and garlic, mixing thoroughly after each addition. If the mixture is too thick, add more of the cooking water. Fold in salt, pepper, cilantro, and butter, if using. Serve immediately.

Serves 4 to 5

PER SERVING: 108 calories, 3 g protein, 23 g carbohydrate, 1 g total fat (trace saturated fat, trace mono, trace poly fat), 0 mg cholesterol, 2 g dietary fiber, 4 RE vitamin A, 12 mcg folate, 15 mg vitamin C, 6 mg sodium, 427 mg potassium, 1 mg iron, 16 mg calcium

**Variation:**

For a slightly richer sauce, substitute ½ cup of milk for ½ cup of cooking water.

# Oven-Roasted Herbed Potatoes and Tofu

POTATOES ARE SUCH a versatile food, and this is one of the tastiest ways to serve them.

|         |                                                   |
|---------|---------------------------------------------------|
| 4       | large potatoes, peeled, cut into bite-sized pieces |
| ½ cup   | cubed extra-firm tofu                             |
| I tbsp. | chopped fresh parsley *or* cilantro               |
| I tbsp. | chopped fresh dill                                |
| 2       | garlic cloves, minced                             |
| ½ tsp.  | dried oregano                                     |
|         | chili pepper flakes (optional)                    |
| 4 tbsp. | olive oil                                         |
|         | salt, to taste                                    |

Preheat oven to 400°F.

Pour potatoes and tofu into a container with a lid. Container should be only half full. Add herbs, garlic, pepper, and oil. Cover with lid and shake gently so that potatoes and tofu become evenly coated with herbs and oil.

Arrange potatoes and tofu in a single layer on a cookie sheet. Bake about 30 minutes, turning once halfway through. Potatoes and tofu will be just lightly golden. If more browning is desired, turn oven to broil and place cookie sheet on top rack for 3 to 5 minutes. Sprinkle with salt just before serving.

Serves 4 to 6

PER SERVING: 210 calories, 6 g protein, 24 g carbohydrate, 11 g total fat (2 g saturated fat, 7 g mono, 2 g poly fat), 0 mg cholesterol, 3 g dietary fiber, 8 RE vitamin A, 19 mcg folate, 16 mg vitamin C, 8 mg sodium, 489 mg potassium, 3 mg iron, 54 mg calcium

**Variations:**

Substitute sweet potatoes for potatoes. Add sliced carrots and/or corn to the potatoes and tofu; wrap them in aluminum foil and cook them on the grill or barbecue for about 30 minutes. Delicious!

# Baked Potato Croquettes

CROQUETTES ARE FLAVORFUL mixtures of minced vegetables or meat, seasonings and a thick white sauce formed into small balls or cylinders, then breaded and fried or baked. These are a tasty, healthy and low-fat version.

| | |
|---|---|
| 3 tbsp. | *each*, wheat germ and bread crumbs |
| 4–5 | medium potatoes, peeled, cooked, mashed |
| ½ cup | grated Cheddar *or* Gruyère cheese |
| ½ cup | grated firm tofu |
| I tbsp. | flour |
| I | egg, beaten |
| ¼ tsp. | dry mustard |
| I tbsp. | chopped fresh cilantro *or* parsley |
| | generous pinch, *each*, dried oregano and tarragon |
| | generous pinch dried chili peppers (optional) |

Mix wheat germ and bread crumbs on a plate. Set aside.

Combine potatoes, cheese and tofu. Add flour, egg, and mustard. Mix in herbs and seasonings. When mixture is smooth, shape into 2-inch long croquettes, using about 2 tbsp. for each.

Roll croquettes in crumb mixture. Place on greased cookie sheet. Bake at 400°F for 15 minutes. To brown tops, broil 3 to 5 minutes.

Makes 18 to 24 croquettes

PER CROQUETTE: 53 calories, 3 g protein, 7 g carbohydrate, 2 g total fat (I g saturated fat, trace mono, trace poly fat), 11 mg cholesterol, I g dietary fiber, 12 RE vitamin A, 9 mcg folate, 4 mg vitamin C, 27 mg sodium, 136 mg potassium, I mg iron, 33 mg calcium

**Variations:**

Croquettes can be pan fried in a little vegetable oil instead of baked.

# Couscous Croquettes

ENJOY THESE AS a side dish or simply with your favorite dip and a salad—they're especially good with homemade Aïoli (p. 62). Couscous, a very fine granular pasta made from semolina, is a North African staple that is now very popular in North America. Sold in large supermarkets and health food stores, it comes in several varieties, including quick-cooking versions. Cook according to package directions. Herbes de Provence usually include basil, fennel, marjoram, thyme, rosemary, sage, and summer savory. Italian seasonings usually include marjoram, thyme, rosemary, savory, sage, oregano, and sweet basil.

| | |
|---|---|
| 1 cup | cooked couscous, cooled |
| 2 | eggs, beaten |
| 1 cup | grated Cheddar cheese |
| ½ cup | grated firm tofu |
| 2 tbsp. | bread crumbs |
| ¼ tsp. | herbes de Provence or Italian seasonings |
| | salt and pepper, to taste |
| | oil for frying (enough to cover croquettes) |

In a medium bowl, combine all ingredients, except oil, until mixture is of a uniform consistency. Shape into 16 equal-sized balls. If mixture is too sticky to shape, add a few more bread crumbs. Cover and let rest for 30 minutes.

Heat oil in a wok or deep-frying pan. Gently drop croquettes into hot oil and fry 5 to 7 minutes, or until evenly crisp and golden. Drain on paper towels; keep warm until ready to serve.

Croquettes can be made a day ahead. Reheat in a regular oven to maintain crispness.

Makes about 16

PER CROQUETTE: 65 calories, 4 g protein, 4 g carbohydrate, 4 g total fat (2 g saturated fat, 1 g mono, 1 g poly fat), 34 mg cholesterol, .3 dietary fiber, 35 RE vitamin A, 8 mcg folate, trace vitamin C, 66 mg sodium, 42 mg potassium, 1 mg iron, 73 mg calcium

# Mango Couscous

REFRESHING AND EASY to prepare, Mango Couscous is suitable as either a side dish with dinner or as a main dish for lunch. Serve it with a salad or grilled vegetables.

| | |
|---|---|
| ½ cup | uncooked couscous |
| 2 tbsp. | raisins |
| 1 tbsp. | vegetable oil |
| 1 | medium onion, thinly sliced |
| 1 tbsp. | granulated sugar |
| ½ cup | cubed firm *or* extra-firm tofu |
| 2 tbsp. | chopped cashews |
| | salt and pepper, to taste |
| 1 | mango, peeled and cut into small cubes |

In a large pot, cook couscous according to package directions. When done, fold in raisins. Cover and set aside.

In a small, nonstick frying pan, heat oil. Add onions and sugar. Caramelize onions by cooking them over low heat for about 30 minutes, stirring often. (This can be done several hours ahead.)

Stir onions, tofu, cashews, salt, and pepper into couscous/raisin mixture. Heat through. Fold in mango cubes.

Serves 3 as a main dish, 5 as a side dish

PER SIDE DISH SERVING: 208 calories, 8 g protein, 30 g carbohydrate, 7 g total fat (1 g saturated fat, 3 g mono, 3 g poly fat), 0 mg cholesterol, 2 g dietary fiber, 6 RE vitamin A, 24 mcg folate, 10 mg vitamin C, 31 mg sodium, 220 mg potassium, 3 mg iron, 74 mg calcium

**Variations:**

Instead of mango, try fresh peaches or apricots.

# Thai-Style Breaded Tofu Fries

THE ZESTY THAI MARINADE and crunchy coating make these low-fat, oven-baked tofu fries a healthy alternative to regular fries.

## Thai Marinade

| | |
|---|---|
| 2 tbsp. | minced ginger root |
| 1 | lemon, juice of |
| 2 tbsp. | soy sauce |
| 1 tbsp. | honey |
| 1 tbsp. | roasted sesame oil |
| 2 | garlic cloves, minced |
| | hot pepper flakes, to taste |
| 12.4 oz. | pkg. extra-firm tofu |

## Crumb Mixture

| | |
|---|---|
| ⅓ cup | seasoned bread crumbs |
| ¼ cup | wheat germ |
| 2 tbsp. | sesame seeds |

In a small saucepan, combine Thai Marinade ingredients. Stir over low heat until honey has melted. Set aside.

Cut tofu into strips resembling French fries. Arrange strips in a bowl. Pour Thai Marinade over strips. Cover and let marinate 2 to 6 hours.

Preheat oven to 350°F.

Combine crumb mixture ingredients. Roll tofu strips in crumbs and place on lightly greased nonstick baking sheet.

Bake 8 minutes; turn strips over and bake another 8 minutes, or until strips are golden. Serve with a plum sauce or your favorite dipping sauce.

Serves 4

PER SERVING: 204 calories, 15 g protein, 16 g carbohydrate, 10 g total fat (1 g saturated fat, 3 g mono, 5 g poly fat), 0 mg cholesterol, 2 g dietary fiber, trace vitamin A, 29 mcg folate, 4 mg vitamin C, 346 mg sodium, 133 mg potassium, 3 mg iron, 109 mg calcium

# Cornbread Pudding

FOR A NUTRITIOUS, LIGHT lunch just add a salad to this flavorful dish.

|          |                                          |
|----------|------------------------------------------|
| 1 cup    | soft tofu                                |
| ⅓ cup    | water                                    |
| 2 tbsp.  | honey                                    |
| 3 tbsp.  | vegetable oil                            |
| 1        | egg                                      |
| 1        | egg white                                |
| 2 cups   | corn kernels, fresh *or* frozen          |
| 2        | green onions, thinly sliced              |
| ½        | red pepper, finely chopped               |
| ½ cup    | grated Cheddar cheese                    |
| ½ cup    | diced medium *or* firm tofu              |
| 1 cup    | cornmeal                                 |
| 2 tsp.   | baking powder                            |
|          | generous pinch dried chili peppers,      |
|          | salt and pepper to taste (optional)      |

Preheat oven to 350°F.

In a large bowl, using an electric hand blender, blend together soft tofu, water, honey, oil, egg, and egg white. Fold in corn kernels, onions, red pepper, cheese, and tofu cubes. Add dry ingredients and seasonings and stir gently until well blended.

Pour into a greased 9" baking dish and bake about 40 minutes, or until a toothpick inserted in center comes out clean. To serve, spoon onto plates or cut into wedges.

Serves 6 to 8

PER SERVING: 338 calories, 10 g protein, 50 g carbohydrate, 12 g total fat (3 g saturated fat, 4 g mono, 4 g poly fat), 34 mg cholesterol, 2 g dietary fiber, 69 RE vitamin A, 25 mcg folate, 5 mg vitamin C, 167 mg sodium, 201 mg potassium, 3 mg iron, 168 mg calcium

# Gnocchis Grenoblois (French-Style Polenta)

I FIRST LEARNED how to make polenta while I was living in Grenoble, France, many years ago. It's a pleasant change from rice or potatoes. Be sure to serve it with gravy.

| | |
|---|---|
| ⅔ cup | cream of wheat |
| ⅓ cup | cornmeal |
| 1½ cups | milk |
| 1 cup | mashed soft tofu |
| ½ | bouillon cube *or* salt and pepper, to taste |
| ⅔ cup | grated Cheddar *or* Swiss cheese |
| ⅓ cup | shredded mozzarella cheese, for topping |

Pour cream of wheat, cornmeal, milk, tofu, and bouillon cube into a medium-sized saucepan. Over medium-high heat, stir constantly until mixture comes to a boil. Reduce heat to low. Add grated cheese and simmer, stirring until mixture is smooth and resembles a thick paste. When mixture detaches itself from the sides and bottom of the pan, it is ready to pour into a greased 8″ square baking dish.

Let cool 2 minutes, then press down gently so that the surface of the gnocchis is smooth. When completely cool, cut into 2½-inch squares in pan and sprinkle with mozzarella. The gnocchis can be made to this point 1 day ahead.

About ½ hour before serving, broil gnocchis in regular oven for 3 to 5 minutes, or until they are golden and the mozzarella is bubbly. Turn oven to warm and let sit 10 to 15 minutes before serving. Gnocchis can also be heated in the microwave oven, about 3 minutes on high, or until cheese is bubbly.

Serves 5 to 6

PER SERVING: 225 calories, 11 g protein, 27 g carbohydrate, 8 g total fat (4 g saturated fat, 2 g mono, 1 g poly fat), 21 mg cholesterol, 1 g dietary fiber, 95 RE vitamin A, 9 mcg folate, 1 mg vitamin C, 228 mg sodium, 138 mg potassium, 2 mg iron, 223 mg calcium

# Spaetzle

THIS SPECIALTY FROM southern Germany is a type of homemade fresh pasta or miniature dumpling. Spaetzle are to southern Germans what French fries are to the French. Traditionally served with gravy, they can also be tossed with a little butter and grated cheese, such as Cheddar, Swiss, and so on.

| | |
|---:|:---|
| ½ cup | mashed soft tofu |
| 3 | eggs |
| 2 cups | all-purpose flour |
| I tsp. | salt |
| ¼ cup | water |

In a medium bowl, beat tofu and eggs together with a hand blender. Add flour, salt and water. Using a wooden spoon, beat vigorously until air bubbles form. Batter should be firm and sticky.

Bring 2 quarts water plus 1 tbsp. salt to a boil. Reduce heat to medium.

Place ⅓ of the batter on a cutting board measuring about 6 x 12". Hold one end of cutting board and let other end rest on rim of pot. With a knife, scrape very thin strips of batter into the boiling water. When all the batter has been scraped off, bring water to a rolling boil. Reduce heat to low and stir spaetzle to loosen and separate. Cook 1 minute longer, then remove spaetzle with a slotted spoon and pour into colander. Rinse with hot water to prevent sticking. Transfer to a serving dish and keep warm.

Repeat cooking procedure until all batter is used. Spaetzle can be served immediately or covered and refrigerated for up to 2 days.

If preparing spaetzle in advance, reheat in microwave oven or in boiling salted water. To serve leftover spaetzle, pan fry them in a little butter.

Serves 4 to 6

PER SERVING: 194 calories, 8 g protein, 32 g carbohydrate, 3 g total fat (1 g saturated fat, 1 g mono, 1 g poly fat), 106 mg cholesterol, 1 g dietary fiber, 48 RE vitamin A, 23 mcg folate, 0 mg vitamin C, 421 mg sodium, 70 mg potassium, 2 mg iron, 22 mg calcium

# Herbed Bread Pancakes

QUICK, EASY TO prepare and nutritious; these are great on their own or as a side dish.

| | |
|---:|:---|
| 4 oz. | leftover bread (the equivalent of 2 Italian buns), cut up |
| ½–1 cup | milk, depending on dryness of bread |
| 1 tbsp. | vegetable oil |
| 1 | medium onion, finely chopped |
| ½ cup | mashed medium tofu |
| 2 | eggs, beaten |
| 1 tbsp. | unbleached flour |
| 1 tbsp. | *each*, chopped fresh parsley and basil |
| | generous pinch dried tarragon |
| | salt and pepper, to taste |

Place bread in a medium bowl. Pour milk over it and let sit 15 minutes, until milk is absorbed and bread is moist.

Meanwhile, in a small frying pan, heat oil; sauté onions until translucent and starting to brown, 4 to 5 minutes. Set aside.

Add tofu, eggs, and flour to the bread and milk. Mash with a fork. Mix in onions, herbs, salt, and pepper.

Heat a large, lightly greased nonstick frying pan over medium heat. Drop 2 heaping tbsp. of batter per pancake into the hot pan, spreading the mixture with the back of a fork so that it is about ½-inch thick. Cook in batches of 3 or 4 about 3 minutes per side, or until lightly browned. Serve warm.

Herbed bread pancakes can be made ahead and reheated in a microwave oven just before serving.

Serves 4, or makes about 10 pancakes

PER PANCAKE: 80 calories, 4 g protein, 8 g carbohydrate, 4 g total fat (1 g saturated fat, 1 g mono, 1 g poly fat), 43 mg cholesterol, 1 g dietary fiber, 31 RE vitamin A, 14 mcg folate, 2 mg vitamin C, 78 mg sodium, 82 mg potassium, 1 mg iron, 52 mg calcium

# MEATLESS MAIN DISHES

# Grilled Peppers, Mushrooms, and Tofu

LIGHT, HEALTHY AND flavorful, you can enjoy this dish all year round—on the barbecue in the summer and on the indoor grill in the winter.

| | |
|---|---|
| 1 | *each*, green, orange and red peppers, quartered |
| 8 | medium whole mushrooms |
| 12.4 oz. | pkg. firm *or* extra-firm tofu, cut into ½-inch thick slices |
| 6 tbsp. | All-Purpose Salad Dressing (p. 80), *or* to taste |

Brush both sides of peppers, mushrooms, and tofu slices with salad dressing. Arrange in a large bowl, cover, and let marinate 2 to 6 hours.

Drain marinade from peppers, mushrooms, and tofu and reserve.

Over high heat, grill or barbecue peppers, mushrooms, and tofu. Brush with reserved marinade during cooking; grill about 5 minutes on each side, or until browned. Serve over rice, couscous, or pasta.

Serves 4

PER SERVING: 216 calories, 16 g protein, 9 g carbohydrate, 15 g total fat (2 g saturated fat, 7 g mono, 5 g poly fat), 0 mg cholesterol, 4 g dietary fiber, 52 RE vitamin A, 32 mcg folate, 99 mg vitamin C, 89 mg sodium, 535 mg potassium, 10 mg iron, 195 mg calcium

**Variations:**

Try a medley of grilled vegetables, such as mushrooms, zucchini, eggplant and onions.

**NOTE:** Grilling time can vary considerably, depending on the type of grill used. Electric grills, for example, do not get as hot as regular barbecue grills.

# Sautéed Tofu in Coconut Curry Sauce

COCONUT MILK AND curry powder give tofu a wonderfully smooth texture with a burst of flavor. I use the medium custardlike tofu for this dish, even though the soft cubes may break up during cooking.

| | |
|---|---|
| 2 tbsp. | roasted sesame oil, divided |
| 1 lb. | medium *or* firm tofu, cubed |
| | salt and pepper, to taste |
| 2 | green onions, chopped |
| 1 | red pepper, julienned |
| 1 | large zucchini, cut into 2" strips |
| | hot pepper flakes, to taste (optional) |
| 1 tbsp. | curry powder |
| ½ cup | canned unsweetened coconut milk |
| ½ cup | vegetable *or* chicken broth |
| 2 tbsp. | roasted sesame seeds |
| 2 tbsp. | chopped cashew nuts |
| 2 tbsp. | shredded basil leaves |

Heat 1 tbsp. of the oil in a nonstick wok or deep frying pan. Over high heat, sauté the tofu 1 to 2 minutes, or until lightly golden. Sprinkle with salt and pepper. Transfer tofu to dish and set aside.

Add remaining 1 tbsp. oil to wok and, over high heat, sauté onions, peppers, and zucchini 2 to 3 minutes. Sprinkle with hot pepper flakes, if using, and fold in curry powder, coconut milk, broth, and tofu. Cook until mixture is heated through. Adjust seasonings. Stir in sesame seeds, cashews, and basil. Serve over rice or noodles.

Serves 4

PER SERVING: 284 calories, 13 g protein, 9 g carbohydrate, 24 g total fat (9 g saturated fat, 6 g mono, 7 g poly fat), 0 mg cholesterol, 4 g dietary fiber, 35 RE vitamin A, 41 mcg folate, 22 mg vitamin C, 113 mg sodium, 408 mg potassium, 8 mg iron, 186 mg calcium

# Five-Minute Sweet and Sour Tofu Stir-Fry

IF YOU LIKE CHINESE food, you must try this quick and easy dish which is both light and nutritious.

| | |
|---|---|
| 2 tbsp. | vegetable oil |
| 1 | medium onion, coarsely chopped |
| 1 | red pepper, julienned |
| ½ | green pepper, julienned |
| 1 lb. | medium *or* firm tofu, cut into bite-sized pieces |
| | salt and pepper, to taste |
| 16 oz. | jar sweet and sour sauce, commercial or 1 recipe Basic Sweet and Sour Sauce (see following) |

Over high heat, in a wok or other deep nonstick frying pan, heat oil. Add onions and peppers and stir-fry 2 minutes. Add tofu and continue to stir-fry 1 minute. Sprinkle with salt and pepper. Fold in sweet and sour sauce. Reduce heat to medium and cook until heated through. Serve over rice or Chinese noodles.

If you'd like to make your own sweet and sour sauce, the following recipe will take another 5 minutes to prepare.

Serves 4

PER SERVING: 340 calories, 10 g protein, 52 g carbohydrate, 13 g total fat (2 g saturated fat, 4 g mono, 6 g poly fat), 0 mg cholesterol, 3 g dietary fiber, 68 RE vitamin A, 37 mcg folate, 37 mg vitamin C, 426 mg sodium, 555 mg potassium, 7 mg iron, 171 mg calcium

# Basic Sweet and Sour Sauce

USE THIS VERSATILE tangy sauce in any sweet and sour recipe.

| | |
|---|---|
| ¼–½ cup | white vinegar |
| ½ cup | brown sugar |
| ½ cup | ketchup |
| 8 oz. | can pineapple tidbits with juice |
| 2 tsp. | cornstarch |

In a medium saucepan, combine all ingredients. Over medium heat, stir until mixture comes to a boil. Add desired quantity of sauce to any sautéed vegetables, tofu and/or meat. Cover and refrigerate any leftover sauce for up to 1 week.

Makes about 8 sauce servings, 1 serving = ¼ cup

PER SERVING: 88 calories, trace protein, 23 g carbohydrate, trace total fat (trace saturated fat, trace mono, trace poly fat), 0 mg cholesterol, trace dietary fiber, 18 RE vitamin A, 4 mcg folate, 8 mg vitamin C, 208 mg sodium, 161 mg potassium, 1 mg iron, 19 mg calcium

**Variations:**

For **Hawaiian Chicken or Pork**, just add thin strips of stir-fried chicken or pork to the above stir-fry and sauce. Yummy! Also try shrimp or any firm-fleshed white fish, such as cod or halibut.

# Greek Pasta with Beans, Tomatoes, and Feta

THIS IS ONE of the many recipes my daughter Bettina has tested for me. She enjoyed it so much that she has made it many times since then for family and friends.

| | |
|---|---|
| 2 cups | uncooked pasta (penne *or* rotini) |
| 1 tbsp. | vegetable oil |
| ½ | medium onion, coarsely chopped |
| 2–3 | garlic cloves, minced |
| 4 | sun-dried tomatoes, in oil, drained, coarsely chopped |
| 19 fl. oz. | can stewed tomatoes, drained, liquid reserved |
| 19 fl. oz. | can white beans, rinsed and drained |
| 2 tbsp. | chopped fresh basil, cilantro, *or* parsley, *or* a combination |
| | generous pinch dried oregano |
| | salt *or* soy sauce, to taste |
| dash | cayenne pepper (optional) |
| 10 oz. | bag fresh spinach, shredded |
| 2 tbsp. | sliced black olives *or* 8–10 whole olives |
| 1 cup | cubed medium *or* firm tofu |
| ½ cup | crumbled feta cheese |

Cook pasta according to package directions. Drain, keep warm.

In a large, deep, nonstick frying pan, heat oil. Add onion, garlic, and sun-dried tomatoes. Sauté 1 or 2 minutes. Add stewed tomatoes, beans, herbs, and seasonings. Simmer on low about 5 minutes. If mixture is dry, stir in some liquid from the stewed tomatoes. Add spinach. Cover and simmer another 3 to 5 minutes, or until spinach is wilted. Fold in olives and tofu. Adjust seasonings.

Serve tomato/bean mixture over the hot pasta; top with feta.

Serves 4 to 5

PER SERVING: 393 calories, 19 g protein, 47 g carbohydrate, 19 g total fat (5 g saturated fat, 8 g mono, 4 g poly fat), 23 mg cholesterol, 10 g dietary fiber, 559 RE vitamin A, 140 mcg folate, 72 mg vitamin C, 1051 mg sodium, 1343 mg potassium, 8 mg iron, 338 mg calcium

# Beans, Lentils, and Tofu in Spicy Tomato Sauce

YOU CAN WHIP up this flavorful dish in a flash if you keep a few cans of lentils and tomato sauce handy in your kitchen cupboard. There is no added fat, making this healthy dish almost fat free.

| | |
|---|---|
| 19 fl oz. | can lentils, drained and rinsed |
| 19 fl oz. | can white beans, drained and rinsed |
| 19 fl oz. | can tomato sauce |
| 2 | medium ripe tomatoes, chopped |
| 1 | medium onion, chopped |
| 2 | garlic cloves, minced |
| 2 tbsp. | chopped fresh herbs |
| | generous pinch dried oregano |
| | soy sauce and hot pepper sauce, to taste |
| 1 cup | cubed medium *or* firm tofu |

In a large saucepan, combine all ingredients. Cover and simmer over low heat for about 30 minutes, stirring occasionally. If tomatoes are very juicy, remove lid and continue to simmer until liquids have evaporated. Serve over rice, pasta or couscous.

Serves 4

PER SERVING: 242 calories, 19 g protein, 46 g carbohydrate, 4 g total fat (1 g saturated fat, 1 g mono, 2 g poly fat), 0 mg cholesterol, 11 g dietary fiber, 188 RE vitamin A, 66 mcg folate, 27 mg vitamin C, 1576 mg sodium, 1309 mg potassium, 7 mg iron, 175 mg calcium

**Variation:**

For a **Meatless Tofu Chili**, omit herbs and soy sauce. Add a dash of Worcestershire sauce, generous pinches of cumin and cayenne, 1 to 2 tbsp. chili powder, and crushed red pepper flakes to taste. Chopped red and green bell peppers and celery may also be added.

**4** Scallops and Shrimp Provençal, *page 123*

**5** Greek Pasta with Beans, Tomatoes and Feta, *page 113*

**Bunes,** *page 182*

 **Brandy-Soaked Oranges
with Almond Lemon Cream,** *page 153*

# Cheese-filled Manicotti with Tomato Sauce

ALL LOVERS OF Italian food will enjoy this satisfying dish. It can be prepared a day ahead and baked just before serving.

|          |                               |
|---------:|-------------------------------|
| 10–12    | manicotti                     |

### Cheese Filling

|          |                                    |
|---------:|------------------------------------|
| 1 lb.    | low-fat ricotta cheese             |
| 1 cup    | grated extra-firm tofu             |
| 2        | eggs, beaten                       |
| 2 tbsp.  | grated Parmesan cheese             |
| ½ cup    | shredded mozzarella cheese         |
| 1 tbsp.  | chopped fresh cilantro *or* parsley |
|          | salt and pepper, to taste          |
|          |                                    |
| 4 cups   | your favorite tomato sauce         |
| 2 tbsp.  | grated Parmesan cheese             |

Cook manicotti according to package directions. Drain and toss with a small amount of butter or olive oil.

In a medium bowl, combine cheese filling ingredients with a fork. Stuff manicotti with cheese filling.

Spread 1 cup of tomato sauce over bottom of a 9 x 13" baking dish. Arrange stuffed manicotti in a single layer and cover with remaining tomato sauce. Sprinkle with grated Parmesan. Cover loosely with aluminum foil. Bake at 350°F for 20 minutes. Remove foil and continue baking for 15 to 20 minutes, or until tender.

Serves 4 to 6

PER SERVING: 373 calories, 25 g protein, 50 g carbohydrate, 9 g total fat (4 g saturated fat, 1 g mono, 2 g poly fat), 53 mg cholesterol, 4 g dietary fiber, 272 RE vitamin A, 29 mcg folate, 11 mg vitamin C, 1177 mg sodium, 659 mg potassium, 4 mg iron, 266 mg calcium

# Penne Alfredo

THIS HEALTHY, LOW-FAT Alfredo sauce is every bit as satisfying as the traditional rich version. The tofu gives it a creamy texture; the garlic and wine add robust flavor.

| | |
|---|---|
| 2 cups | uncooked penne pasta |
| 4 tbsp. | grated Parmesan cheese, divided |

## Alfredo Sauce

| | |
|---|---|
| ½ cup | soft *or* medium tofu |
| 2 tbsp. | whipping cream |
| ½ cup | dry white wine, divided |
| 2 | garlic cloves, minced |
| 1 tbsp. | chopped fresh parsley |
| | salt and pepper, to taste |

In a large pot, cook penne according to package directions. Drain. Return penne to pot. Sprinkle with 3 tbsp. grated Parmesan cheese. Cover.

In a small bowl, with electric hand blender, blend together tofu, whipping cream, and half of wine. Set aside.

In a small saucepan, simmer remaining wine, garlic, parsley, salt, and pepper for about 3 minutes. Fold in tofu mixture.

Pour Alfredo sauce over penne and cook over low heat until heated through. If sauce is too thick, mix in a little wine or water. Adjust seasonings. Transfer to a serving platter and sprinkle with remaining 1 tbsp. Parmesan cheese. Serve immediately.

Serves 4 to 5

PER SERVING: 217 calories, 8 g protein, 33 g carbohydrate, 4 g total fat (2 g saturated fat, 1 g mono, 1 g poly fat), 10 mg cholesterol, 1 g dietary fiber, 30 RE vitamin A, 9 mcg folate, 1 mg vitamin C, 82 mg sodium, 106 mg potassium, 2 mg iron, 75 mg calcium

**Variations:**

To the above recipe, add ½ cup of 1 of the following: cubed, medium *or* firm tofu; sautéed sliced mushrooms; chopped ham; crab meat or baby shrimp.

# Macaroni and Cheese

AN ALL-TIME favorite comfort food, macaroni and cheese is so easy to make from scratch and so much tastier and more nutritious than the packaged variety.

|  | |
|---|---|
| 2 cups | elbow macaroni |
| 2 cups | Béchamel Sauce (p. 66) |
| I cup + 2 tbsp. | grated Cheddar |
| ½–I cup | milk |
|  | generous pinch dried tarragon |
|  | pepper, to taste |
| ½ cup | cubed firm tofu |
| I tbsp. | bread crumbs |
| I tbsp. | rolled oats |
| I tsp. | butter (optional) |

Cook macaroni in boiling water until just tender. Do not overcook as it will continue to cook in the oven. Drain and set aside.

Meanwhile, make Béchamel sauce. To it add 1 cup grated Cheddar and enough milk to reach the desired consistency. Fold in tarragon and pepper.

Transfer macaroni into an 8–cup casserole. Fold in cubed tofu. Pour cheese sauce over it, stirring gently to make sure all the macaroni is coated.

Combine bread crumbs and oats and sprinkle over macaroni. Dot with butter, if using. Top with remaining Cheddar. Bake at 375°F for 20 to 30 minutes, or until top and edges are starting to brown.

Serves 4 to 6

> PER SERVING: 316 calories, 17 g protein, 36 g carbohydrate, 11 g total fat (6 g saturated fat, 3 g mono, 2 g poly fat), 27 mg cholesterol, 1 g dietary fiber, 103 RE vitamin A, 20 mcg folate, 1 mg vitamin C, 345 mg sodium, 233 mg potassium, 4 mg iron, 284 mg calcium

**Variations:**

For a heartier meal, add ½ cup chopped ham and ½ cup sliced mushrooms to the cheese sauce before pouring it over the macaroni.

# Chinese Noodle Frittata

**DON'T KNOW WHAT** to make for dinner tonight? I bet you have all the ingredients you need for this tasty frittata.

| | |
|---|---|
| 3 oz. | pkg. **Chinese noodle soup mix** |
| I tbsp. | **Garlic Butter** (p. 54) *or* vegetable oil |
| 4 | large **mushrooms**, sliced |
| I | small **onion**, sliced |
| 2 | medium **tomatoes**, chopped |
| 2 tbsp. | chopped fresh **herbs**, divided |
| I cup | cubed medium *or* firm **tofu** |
| | salt, to taste |
| | cayenne pepper, to taste |
| ½ cup | shredded **cheese** (Cheddar, Provolone, *or* Swiss) |
| 3 | **eggs** |
| ¼ cup | **milk** |

Prepare noodles according to package directions. Drain and set aside.

In a large nonstick frying pan, heat **Garlic Butter**. Add mushrooms and onions and sauté over high heat 3 to 4 minutes, until golden. Add tomatoes and 1 tbsp. of herbs and sauté another 2 minutes. Remove from heat. Fold in noodles and tofu, arranging evenly in pan. Sprinkle with salt, pepper and cheese.

In a small bowl, whisk together eggs and milk. Pour evenly over noodle mixture. Sprinkle with remaining herbs. Cover and cook over low heat for 10 to 15 minutes, or until frittata is puffy and just set.

Loosen frittata with a spatula before cutting it into wedges.

Serves 4

PER SERVING: 250 calories, 16 g protein, 13 g carbohydrate, 16 g total fat (5 g saturated fat, 5 g mono, 4 g poly fat), 182 mg cholesterol, 2 g dietary fiber, 171 RE vitamin A, 47 mcg folate, 14 mg vitamin C, 635 mg sodium, 378 mg potassium, 5 mg iron, 217 mg calcium

# Spinach and Cheese Strata

THIS EASY-TO-PREPARE dish is deliciously light and suitable for either lunch or dinner. It puffs up like a soufflé and should be served right out of the oven, before it deflates. Other vegetables, such as sliced mushrooms, peas, corn, and asparagus tips can be substituted for spinach in the filling.

| | |
|---:|:---|
| 8 slices | white *or* 60% whole-wheat bread, crusts removed |
| 10 oz. | pkg. fresh *or* frozen spinach |
| 3 tbsp. | feta cheese |
| 1 cup | soft *or* medium tofu, divided |
| 1 cup | grated Cheddar, divided |
| 3 | eggs |
| 2 cups | milk |
| | salt and pepper, to taste |

Lightly grease bottom and sides of an 8″ square baking dish. Line bottom with 4 slices of bread.

Cook spinach according to package directions. If using fresh, cook in ½ cup boiling water for 5 minutes. Pour into sieve to drain. Squeeze out excess water when cool.

In a medium bowl break up feta with a fork; mix with ½ cup tofu. Fold in spinach. Spread spinach mixture evenly over bread. Sprinkle with half the Cheddar. Cover with the other 4 bread slices. Sprinkle with remaining Cheddar.

In a medium bowl, beat the remaining ½ cup tofu, eggs, milk, salt, and pepper until smooth. Pour gently over bread and Cheddar. Cover and let sit at least 2 hours. Can be stored in refrigerator overnight.

Bake, uncovered, at 350°F for about 45 minutes, or until strata is golden and puffy. Cut into squares. Serve immediately.

Serves 4 to 6

PER SERVING: 285 calories, 17 g protein, 24 g carbohydrate, 14 g total fat (7 g saturated fat, 4 g mono, 1 g poly fat), 139 mg cholesterol, 2 g dietary fiber, 529 RE vitamin A, 83 mcg folate, 7 mg vitamin C, 491 mg sodium, 357 mg potassium, 2 mg iron, 403 mg calcium

# FISH AND MEAT MAIN DISHES

# Scallops Provençal

LA PROVENCE, A picturesque region of southern France, is especially known for its excellent cuisine. Cooking "Provençal style" means cooking with an abundance of fresh herbs, garlic and ripe tomatoes, for intense natural good flavor. Use both scallops and shrimp or just shrimp.

| | |
|---|---|
| 2 tbsp. | vegetable oil |
| ½ | medium onion, chopped |
| 4–6 | garlic cloves, minced |
| I cup | sliced mushrooms |
| I cup | cubed firm or extra-firm tofu |
| 14–18 | ripe cherry tomatoes, halved |
| ¼ cup | raw or roasted red or yellow peppers, julienned |
| ⅓ cup | whole black olives |
| 3 tbsp. | chopped fresh cilantro or parsley |
| ½–I tsp. | Provençal or Italian seasonings |
| | soy sauce, to taste |
| | pepper, to taste |
| ½ cup | medium dry white wine |
| I tsp. | cornstarch |
| 24 | large sea scallops |

In a large, deep, nonstick frying pan, heat oil over high heat. Add onions, garlic, mushrooms, and tofu; sauté until golden, 3 to 5 minutes. Add tomatoes, peppers, olives, herbs, and seasonings and sauté another 1 to 2 minutes.

Combine wine and cornstarch and stir into vegetables. Fold in scallops. Reduce heat to low and let simmer 2 to 4 minutes, turning the scallops once. Do not overcook! Scallops should be soft when cut into, not rubbery. Adjust seasonings. Add a little more wine, if desired. Serve over rice, pasta or couscous.

Serves 4

PER SERVING: 391 calories, 42 g protein, 15 g carbohydrate, 17 g total fat (2 g saturated fat, 7 g mono, 7 g poly fat), 59 mg cholesterol, 3 g dietary fiber, 111 RE vitamin A, 67 mcg folate, 25 mg vitamin C, 627 mg sodium, 1003 mg potassium, 8 mg iron, 203 mg calcium

# Grilled Shrimp, Scallops, and Tofu Kebabs

ONE OF MY favorite dishes, this one is easy to make and the herb/garlic marinade really enhances the natural seafood flavors.

**4   12" wooden skewers**

### Lemon Garlic Marinade

| | |
|---|---|
| **2** | **lemons, juice of** |
| **2 tbsp.** | **olive oil** |
| **2–3** | **large garlic cloves, minced** |
| **½ tsp.** | **dried oregano** |
| **I tbsp.** | ***each*, finely chopped fresh dill, parsley, and basil** |

| | |
|---|---|
| **12** | **large peeled shrimp** |
| **12** | **large sea scallops** |
| **12** | **I" cubes extra-firm tofu** |
| | **salt and pepper, to taste** |

Soak skewers in water for 15 minutes. In a small bowl, combine marinade ingredients.

Thread 3 shrimp, 3 scallops, and 3 tofu cubes, alternating shrimp. scallops, and tofu cubes, on each skewer. Place skewers in a large baking dish and spoon half of marinade over them. Turn skewers and spoon over remaining marinade. Cover and refrigerate 3 to 6 hours.

Just before grilling, sprinkle with salt and pepper. Place skewers on hot grill, about 5 minutes per side, or until shrimp turn pink. (Grilling time can vary, depending on the type of grill used; electric grills, for example, do not get as hot as regular barbecue grills.) Brush kebabs with remaining marinade during grilling time.

Serve with buttered noodles and steamed vegetables.

Serves 4

PER SERVING: 267 calories, 31 g protein, 7 g carbohydrate, 13 g total fat (2 g saturated fat, 6 g mono, 4 g poly fat), 62 mg cholesterol, .2 g dietary fiber, 35 RE vitamin A, 22 mcg folate, 19 mg vitamin C, 188 mg sodium, 385 mg potassium, 3 mg iron, 85 mg calcium

# Poached Salmon with Dill and Garlic Sauce

POACHED SALMON IS always an elegant dish, appreciated by most seafood lovers. The brine is the secret to succulent tasting poached fish.

### Tangy Dill and Garlic Sauce

| | |
|---|---|
| ½ cup | soft or medium tofu |
| ½ cup | plain low-fat yogurt |
| 2 tbsp. | sour cream (optional) |
| 2 tbsp. | fresh lemon juice |
| 2 | garlic cloves, minced |
| 2 tbsp. | coarsely chopped fresh dill |
| | salt and pepper, to taste |

### Brine

| | |
|---|---|
| | water for poaching |
| ½ | medium onion, thinly sliced |
| 3 | garlic cloves, thinly sliced |
| 1 | large carrot, thinly sliced using a vegetable peeler or mandoline |
| 1 | lemon, juice and rind of |
| 8–10 | peppercorns |
| 2 | bay leaves |
| | small bunch parsley, stems removed |
| 1½ lb. | salmon fillet |

**TO MAKE DILL SAUCE:** With electric hand blender, blend together tofu, yogurt, sour cream (if using), and lemon juice until smooth. Fold in garlic, dill, and seasonings. Cover and chill at least 1 hour before serving. Will keep refrigerated up to 3 days.

**TO MAKE BRINE:** Fill a large pot ⅔ full with water. Add all brine ingredients. Bring to a boil. Simmer on low, covered, 20 minutes.

Cut salmon into 4 pieces; leave skin on. Gently drop salmon into brine, making sure it is immersed. If not, add some water. Cover salmon and poach over low heat about 10 minutes. Turn off heat; let salmon sit in hot brine for 10 to 20 minutes.

To serve, remove salmon from brine with a slotted spoon. Discard parsley. Place salmon on a platter and garnish with brine vegetables and sprigs of fresh dill. Serve with **Tangy Dill** and **Garlic Sauce**.

Serves 4; sauce makes 1½ cups, 1 serving = 1 tbsp.

PER SERVING: 224 calories, 35 g protein, 8 g carbohydrate, 6 g total fat (I g saturated fat, 2 g mono, 2 g poly fat), 88 mg cholesterol, I g dietary fiber, 567 RE vitamin A, 12 mcg folate, 24 mg vitamin C, 122 mg sodium, 700 mg potassium, 2 mg iron, 57 mg calcium

PER SAUCE SERVING ONLY: 6 calories, I g protein, I g carbohydrate, trace total fat (trace saturated fat, trace mono, trace poly fat), trace cholesterol, trace dietary fiber, I RE vitamin A, I mcg folate, I mg vitamin C, 5 mg sodium, 18 mg potassium, trace iron, 12 mg calcium

# Fish Cakes

THESE ORANGE ROUGHY fish cakes are low in fat, moist and simply delicious! You can use other fish, such as cod, salmon, or halibut.

| | |
|---:|:---|
| 1 lb. | orange roughy fillets |
| 1 cup | grated extra-firm tofu |
| ½ | medium onion, finely chopped |
| 2 | garlic cloves, minced |
| 2 tbsp. | chopped fresh dill |
| ½ cup | unbleached flour |
| ¼ cup | wheat germ |
| | salt and pepper, to taste |
| | flour to coat fish cakes |

Coarsely chop fish fillets in food processor. Transfer to medium bowl. Stir in remaining ingredients and shape into patties. Coat with flour for easier handling.

In a greased frying pan, over medium heat, pan-fry patties 3 to 5 minutes per side, or until golden. Serve with **Tartar Sauce** (p. 68) or **Aïoli** (p. 62).

Makes 6 large patties

PER PATTY: 176 calories, 20 g protein, 14 g carbohydrate, 5 g total fat (1 g saturated fat, 1 g mono, 2 g poly fat), 15 mg cholesterol, 2 g dietary fiber, 24 RE vitamin A, 33 mcg folate, 1 mg vitamin C, 55 mg sodium, 401 mg potassium, 5 mg iron, 115 mg calcium

# Baked Rainbow Trout

THE TOMATO, ONION, and garlic topping adds a wonderful robust flavor to the trout.

|  |  |
|---|---|
| 4 | medium rainbow trout fillets |
| ½ | lemon, juice of |
| 2 tbsp. | vegetable oil |
| 1 | medium onion, chopped |
| 2 | medium tomatoes, chopped |
| 3 | garlic cloves, minced |
| 2 tbsp. | chopped fresh cilantro *or* parsley |
| 2 tbsp. | chopped sun-dried tomatoes |
| ¼ tsp. | dried oregano |
| ½ | bouillon cube, *or* soy sauce to taste |
|  | pepper, to taste |
| ½ cup | cubed firm tofu |

Arrange trout, skin side down, in lightly greased baking dish. Squeeze lemon over trout. Set aside.

In a medium frying pan, heat oil and add remaining ingredients, except tofu. Sauté over medium heat, about 10 minutes. Fold in tofu. Adjust seasonings. Spread mixture evenly over trout.

Bake, uncovered, at 400°F for 10 to 15 minutes.

Serves 4

PER SERVING: 316 calories, 36 g protein, 9 g carbohydrate, 15 g total fat (2 g saturated fat, 5 g mono, 6 g poly fat), 83 mg cholesterol, 2 g dietary fiber, 88 RE vitamin A, 41 mcg folate, 28 mg vitamin C, 185 mg sodium, 1060 mg potassium, 7 mg iron, 186 mg calcium

**Variations:**

This dish can be made using other fish, such as salmon, halibut, or orange roughy.

# Almond Chicken with Snow Peas and Apricots

THIS IS ONE of my daughter Bettina's favorite dishes. A delicious combination of contrasting flavors—mellow apricots with spicy mustard and soy sauce—enhance the natural good flavor of the chicken and snow peas.

| | |
|---|---|
| 2 tbsp. | vegetable oil, divided |
| 2 | medium chicken breasts (1 whole breast), skin and bone removed, cut into thin strips |
| 2–3 | garlic cloves, minced |
| | salt and pepper, to taste |
| 1 cup | cubed firm tofu |
| 12 | whole almonds |
| ⅓ cup | dried apricots, sliced |
| ½ cup | water |
| ½ cup | apricot preserves |
| 1 tbsp. | Dijon mustard, with seeds |
| | soy sauce, to taste |
| ½ lb. | snow peas |
| 1 tbsp. | roasted sesame seeds |

Heat 1 tbsp. oil in a nonstick wok or frying pan over high heat. Add chicken, garlic, salt, and pepper and stir-fry 2 to 3 minutes. Remove chicken with a slotted spoon; set aside.

Meanwhile, using the same wok, stir-fry cubed tofu in remaining 1 tbsp. oil until golden.

Return chicken to wok. Add almonds, apricots, water, preserves, mustard, and soy sauce. Stir and bring to a boil. Add snow peas and continue to stir-fry another 5 minutes, or until snow peas are just tender crisp. Adjust seasonings. Sprinkle with sesame seeds.

Serves 4 to 5

PER SERVING: 307 calories, 22 g protein, 37 g carbohydrate, 10 g total fat (1 g saturated fat, 4 g mono, 4 g poly fat), 27 mg cholesterol, 4 g dietary fiber, 83 RE vitamin A, 26 mcg folate, 25 mg vitamin C, 118 mg sodium, 458 mg potassium, 7 mg iron, 179 mg calcium

# Stuffed Chicken Breasts with Alfredo Sauce

YOUR FAMILY AND friends should be hungry when you serve them this wonderfully satisfying dish which tastes as good as it looks. You can be sure they'll ask you to make it again!

| | |
|---|---|
| 6 | medium chicken breasts, skin and bone removed (3 whole breasts) |
| | salt and pepper, to taste |

### Spinach Stuffing

| | |
|---|---|
| 10 oz. | pkg. fresh *or* frozen spinach |
| ½ cup | mashed soft *or* medium tofu |
| 3 tbsp. | crumbled feta cheese |
| 1 tsp. | vegetable oil |
| 1 | medium onion, finely chopped |
| 6 tsp. | grated Cheddar cheese |

### Alfredo Sauce

| | |
|---|---|
| 2 cups | Béchamel sauce (p. 66), 1 recipe |
| ¼–½ cup | dry white wine |
| 2 | garlic cloves, minced |

Slightly flatten chicken breasts by placing them between two sheets of wax paper and pounding with a mallet. Sprinkle each side with salt and pepper. Set aside.

Prepare spinach according to package directions. If using fresh, cook in ½ cup boiling water for 5 minutes. Pour into sieve to drain. Squeeze out excess water.

In a medium bowl, combine tofu and feta cheese. Set aside.

Heat oil in a small frying pan. Add onions. Sauté over medium heat until onions are translucent and starting to brown. Remove from heat.

Fold onion and spinach into tofu/feta mixture. Adjust seasonings. Spread over chicken breasts. Top with Cheddar.

Wrap up chicken breasts by pulling up the narrow ends and securing them with a toothpick. Place stuffed breasts in a lightly greased baking dish. Bake at 350°F, uncovered, 15 minutes.

Meanwhile, prepare Béchamel sauce. Add enough wine to obtain the desired thickness. Fold in garlic. Pour sauce over chicken breasts. Continue baking, uncovered, 15 to 20 minutes, or until breasts are cooked through. Do not overcook!

Serve with **Gnocchis Grenoblois** (p. 103), **Spaetzle** (p. 104) or your favorite pasta.

Serves 6

PER SERVING: 415 calories, 60 g protein, 12 g carbohydrate, 11 g total fat (4 g saturated fat, 3 g mono, 2 g poly fat), 159 mg cholesterol, 2 g dietary fiber, 419 RE vitamin A, 67 mcg folate, 8 mg vitamin C, 461 mg sodium, 708 mg potassium, 3 mg iron, 216 mg calcium

ORIGINAL RECIPE PER SERVING: 525 calories, 62 g protein, 7 g carbohydrate, 27 g total fat (15 g saturated fat, 8 g mono, 2 g poly fat), 221 mg cholesterol, 1 g dietary fiber, 422 RE vitamin A, 39 mcg folate, 6 mg vitamin C, 591 mg sodium, 686 mg potassium, 2 mg iron, 257 mg calcium

# Crisp and Tangy Chicken Fingers

SIMPLY DELICIOUS!

| 4 | medium chicken breasts, skin and bone removed (2 whole breasts) |
| | salt and pepper, to taste |

### Herb Garlic Marinade

| ½ cup | medium tofu |
| ½ cup | plain low-fat yogurt |
| 3 | garlic cloves, minced |
| 1–2 tbsp. | chopped fresh dill *or* basil |
| pinch | dried tarragon |
| pinch | crushed red pepper (optional) |
| | salt and pepper, to taste |

### Coating

| ¾ cup | bread *or* cracker crumbs |
| 2 tbsp. | *each*, sesame seeds, wheat, *or* oat bran |
| | oil for deep-frying |

Cut chicken breasts into strips. Sprinkle with salt and pepper.

In a medium bowl, with a hand blender, blend together tofu and yogurt. Stir in remaining marinade ingredients. Fold in chicken strips; coat well. Cover; refrigerate at least 2 hours to overnight.

Combine coating ingredients on a plate. About 1 hour before serving, roll chicken strips in coating mixture.

Using a deep-fryer or wok, heat oil, enough to cover chicken, about 3" deep, to 365°F. Gently drop 6 to 8 chicken fingers into the hot oil. Fry them 7 to 8 minutes, turning once or twice for even browning. Remove chicken fingers with a slotted spoon and drain on paper towels. Place on a serving platter. Keep warm. Repeat until all chicken is done. Serve with your favorite dipping sauce, such as **Aïoli** (p. 62).

Makes 20 to 24 Chicken Fingers

PER CHICKEN FINGER: 46 calories, 6 g protein, 3 g carbohydrate, 1 g total fat (trace saturated fat, trace mono, trace poly fat), 12 mg cholesterol, .2 g dietary fiber, 2 RE vitamin A, 4 mcg folate, trace vitamin C, 46 mg sodium, 82 mg potassium, 1 mg iron, 32 mg calcium

# Tofu Chicken Kebabs with Honey Garlic Peanut Sauce

THE FULL-BODIED flavor of the marinade makes this dish succulent yet low in fat.

4   12" wooden skewers
4   small chicken breasts (2 whole breasts),
    skin and bone removed
8   small mushrooms
12  1" cubes extra-firm tofu

### Honey Garlic Peanut Marinade

2 tbsp.   peanut butter
2 tbsp.   honey
2 tbsp.   Dijon mustard with seeds
3 tbsp.   fresh lemon juice
3         garlic cloves, minced

Soak skewers in water for 15 minutes.

Cut each chicken breast crosswise into 4 equal-sized pieces.

Thread 2 mushrooms, 4 chicken pieces, and 3 tofu cubes, alternating mushrooms, chicken, and tofu, on each skewer, beginning and ending with a mushroom. Place skewers on a platter.

In a small saucepan, combine marinade ingredients. Over low heat, stir until peanut butter and honey have melted. Spoon half of marinade over skewers. Turn skewers and spoon over remaining marinade. Cover and refrigerate 2 to 6 hours.

Place skewers on medium-hot grill about 7 minutes per side, or until chicken is cooked through. (Grilling time can vary considerably depending on the type of grill used.)

Serve over rice pilaf or buttered noodles.

Serves 4

PER SERVING: 324 calories, 42 g protein, 15 g carbohydrate, 11 g total fat (2 g saturated fat, 4 g mono, 5 g poly fat), 69 mg cholesterol, 1 g dietary fiber, 8 RE vitamin A, 17 mcg folate, 8 mg vitamin C, 170 mg sodium, 470 mg potassium, 3 mg iron, 74 mg calcium

# Turkey Stuffing

EVERYONE RAVES ABOUT this turkey stuffing, which my mother used to make for Thanksgiving and Christmas while I was growing up. I am the one preparing turkey dinners for the family now and, although I have tried different kinds of stuffing over the years, this is everybody's favorite. The tofu makes it nice and moist. To roast a stuffed turkey breast up on a rack in an open roasting pan, brush skin with melted butter or vegetable oil and roast at 325°F, 4 hours for 12 lbs., 5½ hours for 16 lbs., or until a meat thermometer inserted into the thickest part of the thigh registers 185°F.

| | |
|---|---|
| 2 | Italian-type crusty buns |
| I cup | milk |
| ½ lb. | lean ground veal |
| ½ lb. | lean ground pork |
| ¼ lb. | sausage meat |
| I | turkey liver, finely chopped |
| 2 | eggs, beaten |
| ½ cup | mashed medium tofu |
| ½ cup | grated extra-firm tofu |
| I | medium onion, finely chopped |
| 2 | garlic cloves, minced |
| 2 tbsp. | chopped fresh herbs such as parsley, cilantro and/or basil |
| | salt and pepper, to taste |

Break bread into large pieces; add milk. When milk is absorbed and bread is soft, break it up with a fork. In a large bowl, combine all ingredients with a fork or your hand. Cover and refrigerate until ready to stuff turkey. Stuffing can be made a day ahead. Once stuffed, the turkey should be cooked immediately to prevent potential food poisoning.

To stuff turkey, spoon stuffing loosely into neck and body cavities. Do not pack down. If any stuffing is left over, shape it into hamburger patties and freeze until ready to use.

For a 12 to 16 lb. turkey, 1 serving = ½ cup

PER SERVING OF STUFFING: 152 calories, 13 g protein, 8 g carbohydrate, 7 g total fat (2 g saturated fat, 2 g mono, 1 g poly fat), 62 mg cholesterol, trace dietary fiber, 29 RE vitamin A, 12 mcg folate, 2 mg vitamin C, 157 mg sodium, 210 mg potassium, 1 mg iron, 60 mg calcium

# Low-Fat Chicken or Turkey Burgers

THESE BURGERS TASTE as "meaty" as regular burgers, yet they have a much lower fat content.

| | |
|---|---|
| 1 lb. | lean ground chicken *or* turkey |
| 1 cup | grated firm tofu |
| ½ | medium onion, finely chopped |
| 1 | garlic clove, minced |
| 2 tbsp. | chopped fresh cilantro *or* other herb(s) |
| 1 | egg white |
| ¼ cup | rolled oats |
| 1 tbsp. | mayonnaise |
| | salt and pepper to taste |

Mix all ingredients in a medium bowl. Shape into burgers. Fry or barbecue as you would regular burgers.

Makes 6 to 8 burgers

PER SERVING: 207 calories, 21 g protein, 4 g carbohydrate, 12 g total fat (3 g saturated fat, 3 g mono, 4 g poly fat), 59 mg cholesterol, 1 g dietary fiber, 8 RE vitamin A, 16 mcg folate, 1 mg vitamin C, 82 mg sodium, 260 mg potassium, 5 mg iron, 83 mg calcium

**Variations:**

Instead of chicken or turkey, try beef, veal, or pork.

# Meatballs with Tomato Sauce

**DON'T LET THE** long list of ingredients prevent you from trying out this easy recipe. Meat combines well with tofu and the oats and wheat germ add fiber to these savory meatballs.

| | |
|---|---|
| 1 lb. | lean ground beef *or* veal *or* combination |
| ½ cup | mashed medium tofu |
| 1 | egg, beaten |
| 2 tbsp. | mayonnaise |
| ¼ cup | rolled oats |
| 2 tbsp. | wheat germ |
| ½ | medium onion, chopped |
| 2 | garlic cloves, minced |
| 2 tbsp. | chopped fresh parsley |
| | generous pinch Italian seasonings |
| | salt and pepper, to taste |
| 6 cups | your favorite tomato sauce |

Combine all ingredients, except for tomato sauce. Shape into 1½-inch meatballs.

In a large, deep, nonstick frying pan, over medium-high heat, brown meatballs. Pour tomato sauce over meatballs and let simmer about 30 minutes.

Makes about 30 meatballs

PER MEATBALL: 72 calories, 4 g protein, 5 g carbohydrate, 4 g total fat (1 g saturated fat, 1 g mono, 1 g poly fat), 19 mg cholesterol, 1 g dietary fiber, 53 RE vitamin A, 10 mcg folate, 3 mg vitamin C, 315 mg sodium, 240 mg potassium, 1 mg iron, 15 mg calcium

# Oven-Roasted Stuffed Zucchini

THE AROMA EMANATING from your kitchen while this dish is roasting in the oven is mouth-watering. Healthy and delicious!

| | |
|---|---|
| 4 | large zucchini, halved lengthwise |
| | salt and pepper, to taste |
| 2 tbsp. | vegetable oil |
| 1 | medium onion, chopped |
| 3–4 | garlic cloves, minced |
| 4 | medium mushrooms, chopped |
| 8 oz. | lean ground meat (beef, chicken *or* veal) |
| 1 cup | cooked rice |
| 3 tbsp. | chopped sun-dried tomatoes |
| 5.5 oz. | can tomato paste |
| 1 cup | grated extra-firm tofu |
| 1 | chicken *or* vegetable bouillon cube |
| 2 tbsp. | chopped, fresh parsley |
| | generous pinch each, cayenne pepper and dried oregano |
| ¼ cup | chopped cashew nuts |
| ½ cup | shredded mozzarella or Cheddar cheese |

Scoop out flesh of zucchini leaving a ½-inch shell; chop flesh coarsely. In a large, lightly greased baking dish, arrange zucchini halves, cut side up, in 1 layer. Sprinkle with salt and pepper. Set aside.

In a large nonstick frying pan, heat oil. Add onions, garlic and mushrooms; stir-fry over medium-high heat for 3 minutes, until lightly browned. Add meat; stir-fry another 3 minutes, until browned. Add chopped zucchini, rice, sun-dried tomatoes, tomato paste, grated tofu, bouillon cube, parsley, cayenne pepper, oregano, and cashews. Stir-fry for 1 minute, combining all ingredients well. Adjust seasonings and remove from heat.

Spoon mixture generously into zucchini shells and sprinkle with cheese. (Any leftover filling can be placed around the zucchini). Cover loosely with foil. (Can be made 1 day ahead to this point).

Bake at 350° for 45 minutes; remove foil and continue baking another 20 minutes, or until zucchini are tender.

Makes 4 to 6 servings

PER SERVING: 338 calories, 19 g protein, 19 g carbohydrate, 21 g total fat (7 g saturated fat, 9 g mono, 4 g poly fat), 38 mg cholesterol, 2 g dietary fiber, 97 RE vitamin A, 24 mcg folate, 22 mg vitamin C, 285 mg sodium, 531 mg potassium, 3 mg iron, 115 mg calcium

# Meat Sauce

MY FAMILY NEVER tires of my meat sauce. It is very flavorful and satisfying and so easy to make. I usually freeze half of it for another day, when I don't have the time to cook.

| | |
|---|---|
| 12–16 oz. | lean ground beef *or* veal |
| ½ | medium onion, chopped |
| 1 | medium carrot, chopped |
| 3–5 | mushrooms, chopped |
| 2 | garlic cloves, minced |
| 1 tbsp. | *each*, chopped fresh cilantro and basil |
| | generous pinch dried oregano |
| 2 tbsp. | rolled oats |
| ⅔ cup | grated firm tofu |
| 5–6 cups | of your favorite tomato sauce |
| ½ tsp. | sugar |
| | salt and pepper, to taste |

In a large, deep, nonstick frying pan, sauté meat and onions 3 to 5 minutes. Add remaining ingredients. Stir and bring to a boil. Reduce heat to low, cover and simmer about 45 minutes. Adjust seasonings. Serve over pasta.

Serves 6

> PER SERVING: 272 calories, 18 g protein, 20 g carbohydrate, 15 g total fat (5 g saturated fat, 6 g mono, 2 g poly fat), 43 mg cholesterol, 4 g dietary fiber, 547 RE vitamin A, 38 mcg folate, 15 mg vitamin C, 1283 mg sodium, 1072 mg potassium, 6 mg iron, 100 mg calcium

**Variations:**

To make **chili**, just add a 16 oz. can of kidney beans, a dash of dried hot chili peppers, 1 to 2 tbsp. chili powder, and a dash of cumin to the above recipe.

# Mixed Bean Chili

IF YOU'RE HUNGRY for something hot and hearty, this flavorful, low-fat chili will definitely hit the spot.

| | |
|---|---|
| ½ lb. | lean ground beef |
| 1 | medium onion, chopped |
| 19 fl. oz. | can mixed beans (or red kidney beans), rinsed and drained |
| ½ cup | grated extra-firm tofu |
| ½–1 cup | cubed extra-firm tofu |
| 1 | yellow or orange pepper, chopped |
| 2 | garlic cloves, minced |
| 2 tbsp. | chopped sun-dried tomatoes |
| 2 tbsp. | chopped fresh parsley |
| 2 tbsp. | rolled oats |
| ½ tsp. | dried oregano |
| pinch | sage |
| ½ tsp. | sugar |
| 5–6 cups | your favorite tomato sauce |
| | salt to taste |
| | hot chili pepper flakes and/or chili powder, to taste |

In a large, deep, nonstick pan, sauté meat and onions for 3 to 5 minutes. Add remaining ingredients. Stir and bring to a boil. Reduce heat to low; cover and simmer about 45 minutes. Adjust seasonings.

Serves 6 to 8

PER SERVING: 253 calories, 16 g protein, 29 g carbohydrate, 9 g total fat (3 g saturated fat, 3 g mono, 2 g poly fat), 23 mg cholesterol, 8 g dietary fiber, 163 RE vitamin A, 87 mcg folate, 56 mg vitamin C, 1175 mg sodium, 994 mg potassium, 3 mg iron, 73 mg calcium

**Variation:**

For **Mixed Bean Vegetarian Chili**, omit ground beef and increase cubed tofu to 1½ cups.

# Rice and Bean Pot

COMFORT FOOD AT its best! Serve this with a salad on a cold day after skiing or a long walk. It can be made ahead and reheated.

|        |                                             |
|--------|---------------------------------------------|
| 2–3    | country-style sausages                      |
| 1 tbsp.| vegetable oil                               |
| 1      | medium onion, chopped                       |
| 6      | medium mushrooms, sliced                    |
| 1 cup  | uncooked brown rice                         |
| 2      | garlic cloves, minced                       |
| 1      | large carrot, sliced                        |
| 1      | large celery stalk, chopped                 |
| ½      | green pepper, chopped                       |
| ½      | red *or* yellow pepper, chopped             |
| 1 cup  | diced extra-firm tofu                       |
| 19 oz. | can kidney *or* other beans, drained        |
| 14 oz. | can stewed tomatoes *or* chunky tomato sauce|
| 1 cup  | chicken *or* beef broth                     |
| 1 tbsp.| chopped fresh cilantro *or* parsley         |
| pinch  | *each*, dried oregano and rosemary          |
|        | salt and pepper, to taste                   |

In a medium saucepan, brown sausages. Cut them into thick slices. Set aside. Pour oil into the same pan and, over high heat, sauté onions and mushrooms, stirring constantly, 2 to 3 minutes, until lightly golden. Add rice and sauté for another minute. Turn into a large casserole.

Pour all other ingredients into casserole, including the sausage slices. Mix and cover. Bake at 350°F for 1 to 1½ hours, or until rice is tender and liquids have been absorbed. Stir and adjust seasonings. Bon appétit!

TOFU MANIA

Serves 4 to 6

PER SERVING: 303 calories, 15 g protein, 45 g carbohydrate, 9 g total fat (2 g saturated fat, 3 g mono, 4 g poly fat), 4 mg cholesterol, 6 g dietary fiber, 403 RE vitamin A, 33 mcg folate, 21 mg vitamin C, 552 mg sodium, 400 mg potassium, 8 mg iron, 140 mg calcium

**Variations:**

For a **Meatless Rice and Bean Pot**, omit the sausages and increase the cubed tofu by ½ cup.

# Pork Tenderloins in Wine Sauce

THIS IS TRULY a dish for the health-conscious gourmet. Pork tenderloins are lean and the accompanying creamy, tasty sauce is low in fat; so enjoy without feeling guilty.

| | |
|---|---|
| 2 x 7 oz. | pkgs. brown gravy mix |
| 3 | garlic cloves, minced |
| 2 tbsp. | *each*, chopped fresh cilantro *or* parsley and dill |
| 1 tsp. | dried oregano |
| ½–1 | chicken bouillon cube |
| 1 cup | soft tofu |
| 1 cup | dry white wine |
| 1 | bay leaf |
| 3 | medium pork tenderloins, fat trimmed |
| | salt and pepper, to taste |
| 1 | medium onion, chopped |
| 8–10 | mushrooms, sliced |

In a medium saucepan, prepare gravy according to package directions. When thickened, stir in garlic, herbs and bouillon cube. In a small bowl, blend tofu and wine together. When smooth, add to gravy. Stir and bring to a boil. Remove from heat. Add bay leaf.

Sprinkle tenderloins with salt and pepper. In a deep, lightly greased, non-stick pan, over medium-high heat, brown tenderloins. When lightly browned, turn over and add onions and mushrooms. Cook until onions and mushrooms are golden.

Pour gravy over tenderloins. Bring to a boil, then reduce heat to low. Cover and simmer for about 1 hour, turning the meat and stirring the sauce occasionally. If the sauce is too thick, add a little wine or water (or both). If it is too thin, add more tofu. To prevent lumping, mix the tofu with 2 to 3 tsp. of gravy and stir well before adding it to the sauce. Adjust seasonings. Remove bay leaf.

To serve, slice each tenderloin into ¾" medallions. The sauce is delicious over a bed of noodles or **Spaetzle** (p. 104).

Serves 4 to 6

PER SERVING: 272 calories, 14 g protein, 48 g carbohydrate, 3 g total fat (1 g saturated fat, 1 g mono, 1 g poly fat), 30 mg cholesterol, 1 g dietary fiber, 7 RE vitamin A, 12 mcg folate, 4 mg vitamin C, 4089 mg sodium, 372 mg potassium, 1 mg iron, 25 mg calcium

# DESSERTS

# Brandy-Soaked Oranges with Almond Lemon Cream

THIS LIGHT AND elegant dessert is so easy to prepare and such a treat for the taste buds! Make it for that next special occasion.

### Brandy-Soaked Oranges

| | |
|---|---|
| 3–4 | large seedless oranges, peeled and sliced crosswise into thin rounds |
| ¼ cup | dried cranberries (optional) |
| 4 tsp. | sugar |
| 4 tbsp. | orange-flavored brandy |
| 2 tbsp. | toasted, sliced almonds |

Arrange overlapping orange slices in 4 layers in a shallow bowl. Sprinkle each layer with ¼ of the cranberries, sugar and brandy. Cover and refrigerate until ready to serve.

Serve orange slices topped with **Almond Lemon Cream** (recipe following) and sprinkled with toasted sliced almonds.

Serves 4 to 6

PER SERVING: 77 calories, I g protein, 14 g carbohydrate, trace total fat (trace g saturated fat, trace mono, trace poly fat), 0 mg cholesterol, 2 g dietary fiber, 19 RE vitamin A, 27 mcg folate, 47 mg vitamin C, trace sodium, 161 mg potassium, trace iron, 35 mg calcium

# Almond Lemon Cream

| | |
|---:|:---|
| ½ cup | whipping cream |
| 3 tbsp. | sugar |
| ½ cup | puréed soft tofu |
| I tbsp. | fresh lemon juice |
| I | lemon, zest of |
| I tbsp. | ground almonds |

Shortly before serving, whip cream and sugar until stiff. Beat in tofu, lemon juice, lemon zest, and ground almonds.

Serves 6

PER SERVING: 116 calories, 2 g protein, 8 g carbohydrate, 9 g total fat (4 g saturated fat, 3 g mono, 1 g poly fat), 23 mg cholesterol, 1 g dietary fiber, 63 RE vitamin A, 4 mcg folate, 4 mg vitamin C, 8 mg sodium, 55 mg potassium, .3 g iron, 30 mg calcium

# No-Bake Lemon Cheesecake Pie

**ATTENTION ALL** cheesecake lovers out there: here is an easy, fat-reduced, no-bake version that is as delicious as a traditional version.

|  |  |
|---|---|
| 8 oz. | ricotta cheese |
| 1 cup | soft *or* medium tofu |
| 14 oz. | can sweetened condensed milk |
| 1½ tsp. | vanilla extract |
| ⅓ cup | fresh lemon juice |
| 2 tsp. | unflavored gelatin |
| 1 | 9" graham cracker crumb crust |

In a medium bowl, with an electric mixer, beat ricotta cheese and tofu until smooth. Gradually beat in condensed milk and vanilla.

Pour lemon juice into a small saucepan. Sprinkle gelatin over juice. Heat over low heat, stirring occasionally until gelatin has dissolved. Fold into cheese/tofu mixture. Pour into pie crust. Cover and chill at least 4 hours or overnight.

Just before serving, top with fresh fruit puree, sliced strawberries, peaches, or berries.

Serves 8

PER SERVING: 372 calories, 10 g protein, 49 g carbohydrate, 16 g total fat (7 g saturated fat, 6 g mono, 3 g poly fat), 31 mg cholesterol, 1 g dietary fiber, 139 RE vitamin A, 12 mcg folate, 6 mg vitamin C, 259 mg sodium, 253 mg potassium, 1 mg iron, 210 mg calcium

# Chilled Strawberry Soufflé with Strawberry Sauce

THIS LIGHT ELEGANT dessert is always a winner. My guests never fail to ask for the recipe!

## Strawberry Sauce

| | |
|---|---|
| 2 lbs. | fresh strawberries, puréed (reserve 3 strawberries for garnish) |
| 1¼ cups | sugar |

## Soufflé

| | |
|---|---|
| ½ cup | water |
| 2 tbsp. | unflavored gelatin (2 pkgs.) |
| 1 cup | whipping cream |
| 1 cup | purèed soft tofu |
| 4 | egg whites |
| 1 tsp. | vanilla extract |

**TO MAKE THE STRAWBERRY SAUCE:** Combine puréed strawberries with sugar. Reserve 2 cups and refrigerate.

**TO MAKE THE SOUFFLÉ:** Pour water into a small saucepan. Sprinkle gelatin over water and heat over low heat until just dissolved. Gently stir into remaining strawberry sauce.

Whip cream and reserve ½ cup for garnish. Beat tofu into remaining whipped cream until smooth.

Beat egg whites until soft peaks form. Fold egg whites, whipped cream, and tofu into strawberry/gelatin mixture. (If this has already set, warm it up just enough to melt the gelatin before mixing it with the egg whites, cream, and tofu.) When smooth, pour into a large decorative glass bowl. Refrigerate and let set at least 2 hours or overnight. When set, garnish with remaining strawberries and whipped cream. Serve with Strawberry Sauce.

Serves 8

PER SERVING: 270 calories, 4 g protein, 42 g carbohydrate, 10 g total fat (6 g saturated fat, 3 g mono, 1 g poly fat), 35 mg cholesterol, 2 g dietary fiber, 98 RE vitamin A, 22 mcg folate, 64 mg vitamin C, 45 mg sodium, 240 mg potassium, 1 mg iron, 42 mg calcium

# Frozen Lemon Cream

LEMON, TOFU, AND cream combine to make a refreshing summer dessert.

|   |   |
|---|---|
| 1 cup | soft tofu |
| 1 cup | whipping cream |
| 1 cup | sugar |
| 2 | fresh lemons, including juice, pulp, and zest |

With hand blender, blend together all ingredients until mixture is smooth and creamy. Pour into freezer container and cover.

Freeze until firm. Remove from freezer 5 minutes before serving.

Makes 5 to 6 servings

PER SERVING: 267 calories, 2 g protein, 39 g carbohydrate, 13 g total fat (8 g saturated fat, 4 g mono, 1 g poly fat), 46 mg cholesterol, 2 g dietary fiber, 128 RE vitamin A, 2 mcg folate, 28 mg vitamin C, 17 mg sodium, 90 mg potassium, 1 mg iron, 54 mg calcium

# Tofu Whipped Topping

IF YOU LIKE whipping cream but feel guilty whenever you eat it, try this lighter version for a change and enjoy!

½ cup    **whipping cream**
I tbsp.   **sugar**
½ cup    **soft or medium tofu, puréed**
I tsp.    **vanilla extract**

Up to 4 hours before serving, whip cream and sugar until stiff. Beat in tofu and vanilla.

Makes 1½ cups, 24 servings, 1 serving = 1 tbsp.

PER SERVING: 19 calories, trace protein, I g carbohydrate, 2 g total fat (I g saturated fat, trace mono, trace poly fat), 6 mg cholesterol, 0 g dietary fiber, 16 RE vitamin A, trace folate, trace vitamin C, 2 mg sodium, 5 mg potassium, trace iron, 4 mg calcium

# Baby Pudding

BECAUSE TOFU IS 95 percent digestible, it is an excellent weaning or geriatric food. Your baby, as well as your elderly parents (and everyone in between!), will enjoy this simple pudding.

| | |
|---|---|
| ¼ cup | water |
| 1½ tbsp. | unflavored gelatin |
| 1 cup | soft or medium tofu |
| 2 cups | milk |
| ⅓ cup | sugar |
| 1 tsp. | vanilla extract |

Pour water into a small saucepan. Sprinkle gelatin over water. Heat over low heat. Stir occasionally until gelatin is dissolved.

Meanwhile, in a medium saucepan, with a hand blender, blend together tofu and milk until smooth. Stir in sugar. Heat over medium–low heat until sugar has dissolved. Do not boil as mixture will curdle when boiled. If this happens, whisk out lumps with hand blender. Remove from heat. Fold in vanilla and gelatin mixture.

Pour into small individual dessert bowls. Cool to room temperature. Cover and refrigerate until set, about 2 hours.

Makes 6 adult servings

PER SERVING: 104 calories, 6 g protein, 16 g carbohydrate, 2 g total fat (1 g saturated fat, 1 g mono, trace poly fat), 6 mg cholesterol, 0 g dietary fiber, 46 RE vitamin A, 4 mcg folate, 1 mg vitamin C, 44 mg sodium, 126 mg potassium, .2 g iron, 104 mg calcium

**Variations:**

For a firmer Jell-O™-type pudding, increase the gelatin by 1½ tsp. Pour gelatin mixture into a lightly greased shallow glass pan, approximately 8 x 12″. Pudding should be about ½-inch deep. When firm, cut jelled pudding into small squares and other shapes.

For flavoring, instead of vanilla, use a few drops of almond extract or 1 tbsp. frozen orange juice concentrate.

# Crème Caramel

THIS LIGHT AND smooth caramelized custard is a perfect ending to any meal. Over the years, I have probably served it to guests more often than any other dessert because it is easy to make and always a hit. Let yourself be tempted by this low-fat version!

| | |
|---|---|
| ½ cup | sugar (to caramelize pudding mold) |
| I cup | milk |
| I cup | soft tofu |
| 3 | eggs |
| ⅓ cup | sugar |
| I tsp. | vanilla extract |

Preheat oven to 300°F.

To caramelize the ½ cup sugar, heat it in a small stainless steel saucepan over medium-high heat. Stir constantly until sugar has completely melted and turned golden. Immediately pour it into an oven-proof, 5–cup pudding mold and turn the mold so that the caramel will coat the sides. Set aside.

Scald the milk.

With a hand blender, blend together tofu, eggs, ⅓ cup sugar, and vanilla until completely smooth. Blend in scalded milk. Pour mixture into prepared caramelized mold and set in a pan of hot water. Poach in oven for about 1 hour 40 minutes. Do not overcook as this causes the custard to be lumpy. Remove from oven. Cool to room temperature, then refrigerate for at least 3 hours or overnight.

To unmold, run a knife around the edges of the custard, then loosen it by gently moving the mold back and forth in a circular fashion. Place a serving platter over the mold, then invert to unmold.

Serves 4 to 6

PER SERVING: 174 calories, 5 g protein, 30 g carbohydrate, 4 g total fat (1 g saturated fat, 1 g mono, 1 g poly fat), 109 mg cholesterol, 0 g dietary fiber, 71 RE vitamin A, 14 mcg folate, trace vitamin C, 53 mg sodium, 94 mg potassium, 1 mg iron, 67 mg calcium

ORIGINAL RECIPE PER SERVING: 480 calories, 6 g protein, 38 g carbohydrate, 34 g total fat (20 g saturated fat, 10 g mono, 2 g poly fat), 289 mg cholesterol, 0 g dietary fiber, 438 RE vitamin A, 25 mcg folate, 1 g vitamin C, 75 mg sodium, 151 mg potassium, 1 mg Iron, 121 mg calcium

# Apple Custard Tart with Brandied Raisins

THIS DELICIOUS TART is definitely worth making. Although it will probably be eaten in one sitting, leftover tart can be refrigerated for up to 3 days.

|  | pastry for 1, 9-inch single pie crust (p. 167) |
|---|---|
| ¼ cup | raisins |
| 2 tbsp. | brandy |
| 3–4 | apples, peeled, sliced |
| 2 tbsp. | sugar |

### Custard Topping

|  |  |
|---|---|
| 1 cup | soft tofu |
| ½ cup | sour cream or plain yogurt |
| 2 tbsp. | orange juice concentrate |
| ¼ cup | sugar |
| 1 tbsp. | flour |
| 1 tbsp. | sliced almonds |
|  | icing (confectioner's) sugar |

Line pie plate with rolled out pastry.

Soak raisins in brandy.

Arrange apple slices in pie shell, overlapping slightly, starting at the outside and working towards the center. Sprinkle apples with 2 tbsp. sugar. Fill in spaces with raisins and brandy.

For custard, using a hand blender, blend together tofu, sour cream, orange juice, sugar, and flour until smooth. Spoon evenly over apples. Sprinkle with almonds.

Bake at 350°F 45 to 50 minutes, or until custard is set and crust is golden. Cool to room temperature. Sprinkle with icing sugar before serving.

Makes 1, 9-inch pie, 8 servings

PER SERVING: 252 calories, 4 g protein, 36 g carbohydrate, 10 g total fat (5 g saturated fat, 3 g mono, 1 g poly fat), 22 mg cholesterol, 1 g dietary fiber, 84 RE vitamin A, 10 mcg folate, 9 mg vitamin C, 211 mg sodium, 166 mg potassium, 1 mg iron, 53 mg calcium

**NOTE:** The nutritional analysis was done using sour cream; yogurt would give significantly lower calorie and fat counts.

**Variations:**

Substitute apricots, peaches or pears for the apples.

# Rhubarb Strawberry Pie

THIS EASY, LOW-FAT pie gets its delicious flavor from the rhubarb and strawberries; it doesn't need the sour cream called for in the original recipe. So, indulge!

|  | pastry for 1, 9-inch single pie crust (p. 167) |
|---|---|
| 3 cups | cubed fresh *or* frozen rhubarb |
| 1 cup | sliced strawberries |
| 1 cup | soft tofu |
| 1 tbsp. | vanilla extract |
| 1 cup | sugar |
| ⅓ cup | unbleached flour |

### Crunchy Brown Sugar Topping
| | |
|---|---|
| 2 tbsp. | *each,* flour, wheat germ, Demerara, *or* brown sugar and melted butter |

Line pie plate with rolled out pastry.

Preheat oven to 350°F.

Place cubed rhubarb and sliced strawberries in a medium bowl.

In a small bowl, with a hand blender, blend together tofu and vanilla extract until smooth. Fold in sugar and flour. Pour mixture over rhubarb and strawberries, stirring gently to coat fruit. Spoon into pie shell.

Combine topping ingredients until crumbly and sprinkle over pie. Bake 45 to 50 minutes, or until fruit is tender and crust is golden. Cool pie to room temperature before cutting into it.

Makes 1, 9-inch pie, 8 servings

PER SERVING: 302 calories, 4 g protein, 49 g carbohydrate, 10 g total fat (6 g saturated fat, 3 g mono, 1 g poly fat), 25 mg cholesterol, 1 g dietary fiber, 90 RE vitamin A, 7 mcg folate, 11 mg vitamin C, 230 mg sodium, 197 mg potassium, 1 mg iron, 75 mg calcium

# Pastry for
# Pies and Quiches

THIS VERSATILE, CRISP, light pastry is suitable for fruit pies and for quiches.

|  |  |
|---|---|
| 2 cups | unbleached flour |
| 1 tsp. | baking powder |
| ¾ tsp. | salt |
| ½ cup | cold butter |
| ¼ cup | grated extra-firm tofu |
| ¼ cup | cold water |

In medium bowl, combine flour, baking powder and salt. Cut in butter with a pastry blender, working quickly so that the butter does not melt. When mixture resembles coarse crumbs, mix in the grated tofu. Add water, using only a small portion at a time until mixture holds together. (More or less water may be needed, depending on the amount of moisture in the tofu).

Divide dough into 2 equal parts. If you are making a single crusted pie, wrap up the second portion and freeze it until ready to use.

Roll out dough on floured board and line pie plate with it. Bake according to pie/quiche recipe directions.

Makes 2 single-crust, 9-inch pie shells or 1 double-crust pie

> PER SINGLE CRUST SERVING (8 servings per pie): 118 calories, 2 g protein, 13 g carbohydrate, 7 g total fat (4 g saturated fat, 2 g mono, trace poly fat), 16 mg cholesterol, 0 g dietary fiber, 57 RE vitamin A, trace folate, 0 mg vitamin C, 194 mg sodium, 19 mg potassium, 1 mg iron, 25 mg calcium

**NOTE:** To bake an unfilled pie shell, line pie plate with pastry; place a sheet of heavy aluminum foil over the pastry, shiny side down. Smooth foil over pastry bottom and let foil edges shield the crust edge. Use raw rice or beans to weigh down the foil. Bake crust at 400°F for 20 minutes. Remove rice or beans and foil. With a fork, prick the crust all over and bake 5 to 10 minutes more, until golden.

# Lemon Squares

THE TANGY FILLING and wholesome crispy crust make these squares a sure hit.

## Brown Sugar Crust

| | |
|---|---|
| 1 cup | unbleached flour |
| ¼ cup | rolled oats |
| 2 tbsp. | wheat germ |
| ½ cup | brown sugar |
| ⅓ cup | butter, softened |

## Lemon Filling

| | |
|---|---|
| 2 | eggs |
| 1 | egg white |
| ½ cup | soft tofu |
| 2 cups | sugar |
| ¼ cup | unbleached flour |
| 1 tsp. | baking powder |
| ½ cup | freshly squeezed lemon juice |
| 2 | lemons, zest of |
| | icing (confectioner's) sugar for sprinkling |

Preheat oven to 350°F.

Lightly grease a 9 x 13" baking dish.

In a large bowl, combine all crust ingredients, using a pastry blender to mix in butter. When mixture is evenly crumbly, press over bottom of baking dish. Bake 15 minutes.

Meanwhile, in a medium bowl, with a hand blender, blend together eggs, egg white and tofu. Add sugar, flour and baking powder and stir until smooth. Gently mix in lemon juice and zest. Pour filling over hot crust.

Bake 30 minutes, or until edges are lightly browned and filling is set. Cool completely before cutting into squares. Sprinkle with icing sugar.

Makes 24 squares

PER SQUARE: 144 calories, 2 g protein, 28 g carbohydrate, 3 g total fat (2 g saturated fat, 1 g mono, trace poly fat), 24 mg cholesterol, .3 g dietary fiber, 31 RE vitamin A, 5 mcg folate, 4 mg vitamin C, 50 mg sodium, 47 mg potassium, 1 mg iron, 24 mg calcium

# Fresh Berry Clafoutis

A CRUSTLESS FRUIT pie of southern France where fresh fruit is so plentiful, clafoutis can be made with any fruit or combination of fruits, e.g., apples, peaches, blueberries, etc. I like it best when made with berries or plums. I've made this recipe with strawberries, but feel free to substitute the freshest berries you can find.

| | |
|---|---|
| ½ cup | butter, at room temperature |
| I cup | sugar |
| 2 | eggs |
| I cup | soft *or* medium tofu |
| I tbsp. | frozen orange juice concentrate |
| I cup | unbleached flour |
| I tsp. | baking powder |
| 2 tbsp. | ground almonds |
| 2 cups | sliced strawberries |
| I tbsp. | fresh lemon juice |
| I tbsp. | slivered almonds |
| I–2 tbsp. | brown sugar |
| | icing (confectioner's) sugar |

In a medium bowl, cream butter and sugar together until smooth.

In a small bowl, with a hand blender, blend together eggs, tofu, and orange juice. Fold into creamed mixture. Add flour, baking powder and ground almonds. Batter should be thick.

Spoon half of batter into a lightly greased 9" pie plate. Spread half of berries evenly over batter. Repeat process. Sprinkle lemon juice, slivered almonds, and brown sugar over berries.

Bake at 350°F for 50 to 60 minutes, or until a toothpick inserted in the center comes out clean. Cool to room temperature. Sprinkle with icing sugar and serve plain or with **Tofu Whipped Topping** (p. 159).

Serves 8

PER SERVING: 396 calories, 5 g protein, 58 g carbohydrate, 17 g total fat (9 g saturated fat, 5 g mono, 1 g poly fat), 86 mg cholesterol, 1 g dietary fiber, 148 RE vitamin A, 12 mcg folate, 19 mg vitamin C, 212 mg sodium, 85 mg potassium, 1 mg iron, 67 mg calcium

Fresh Fruit Clafoutis variation pictured on the front cover.

# Apple Cranberry Crisp

IF YOU'RE IN a hurry but would like to serve a special dessert this evening, this is the one to make. Bake it in the morning; serve it warm or cold any time during the day.

|         |                                                                      |
|--------:|----------------------------------------------------------------------|
| 4       | medium apples, such as **Granny Smith**, peeled, cored, sliced       |
| ½ cup   | cranberries, fresh *or* frozen                                       |
| 4 tbsp. | frozen orange juice concentrate, divided                            |
| 4 tbsp. | sugar, divided                                                       |
| ¼ tsp.  | ground cinnamon                                                      |
| ½ cup   | medium tofu                                                          |
| ½ cup   | plain low-fat yogurt                                                 |
| 1 tbsp. | unbleached flour                                                     |
| 2 tbsp. | *each*, rolled oats, wheat germ, brown sugar and sliced almonds      |

Preheat oven to 400°F.

In a medium bowl, combine apples, cranberries, 2 tbsp. orange juice, 2 tbsp. sugar, and cinnamon. Spread mixture in 8½-inch square shallow baking dish.

In a separate bowl, using a hand blender, blend together tofu, yogurt, flour, remaining orange juice and sugar. Pour evenly over apples and cranberries.

In a small bowl, combine oats, wheat germ and brown sugar. Spoon over apple mixture. Sprinkle with almonds.

Bake 20 to 30 minutes, or until apples are tender.

Serves 4 to 6

PER SERVING: 184 calories, 5 g protein, 37 g carbohydrate, 3 g total fat (trace saturated fat, 1 g mono, 1 g poly fat), trace cholesterol, 3 g dietary fiber, 10 RE vitamin A, 33 mcg folate, 23 mg vitamin C, 41 mg sodium, 324 mg potassium, 2 mg iron, 79 mg calcium

**Variations:**

This is also good with apricots, peaches, or pears.

# Bread Pudding

THIS DELICIOUS BREAD pudding is wonderfully light and puffy. Serve it for dessert or brunch.

| | |
|---|---|
| ½ cup | raisins |
| 2 tbsp. | orange brandy (or other liqueur) |
| 6–8 slices | egg bread, cut into small cubes |
| ½ cup | diced medium or firm tofu |
| 3 | eggs |
| ½ cup | soft tofu |
| ⅓ cup | sugar |
| I tsp. | vanilla extract |
| 2 cups | milk |
| I tsp. | cinnamon |
| 2 tbsp. | brown sugar |

Soak raisins in liqueur for 30 minutes.

Arrange half of the bread cubes in a lightly greased 8–cup baking dish. Spread diced tofu and half of the raisins over bread. Repeat with remaining bread and raisins.

In a medium bowl, with a hand blender, blend together eggs and soft tofu. Add sugar, vanilla, and milk. Blend until smooth. Gently pour mixture over bread and raisins, making sure all the bread is covered. If necessary, press down with a fork. Cover and refrigerate 1 to 4 hours.

About 1½ hours before serving, preheat oven to 350°F.

Sprinkle pudding with cinnamon and brown sugar. Bake for 1 hour, or until puffy and lightly browned. Serve warm with vanilla sauce or ice cream.

Leftover bread pudding tastes delicious cold or warmed up in a microwave oven.

Serves 6 to 8

PER SERVING: 272 calories, 10 g protein, 42 g carbohydrate, 6 g total fat (2 g saturated fat, 2 g mono, 1 g poly fat), 105 mg cholesterol, 2 g dietary fiber, 81 RE vitamin A, 43 mcg folate, 1 mg vitamin C, 256 mg sodium, 265 mg potassium, 3 mg iron, 150 mg calcium

# Carrot Cake

AN IDEAL DESSERT—WHOLESOME, fat- and sugar-reduced, rich in fiber and, above all, scrumptious! I generally use just one cake and freeze the other—for a wonderful impromptu treat.

| | |
|---:|---|
| 3 | eggs |
| ½ cup | soft *or* medium tofu |
| 1¼ cups | brown sugar |
| ¾ cup | canola oil |
| ½ cup | grated extra-firm tofu |
| 1 cup | unbleached flour |
| 1 cup | whole-wheat flour |
| 2 tsp. | *each*, baking powder, baking soda |
| 2 tsp. | ground cinnamon |
| ¼ tsp. | ground cloves |
| ½ cup | raisins |
| ½ cup | chopped walnuts *or* pecans |
| 3 cups | grated carrots |

Grease two 9" round cake pans or one 9 x 13" baking dish.

In a large bowl, with an electric hand blender, blend together eggs and soft tofu. Stir in sugar, oil and grated tofu. Gradually add flours, baking powder, baking soda, cinnamon, and cloves. When batter is well blended, fold in raisins, nuts and grated carrots.

Divide the batter evenly between the two cake pans or spread in baking dish. Bake at 350°F 30 to 40 minutes, or until a toothpick inserted in center comes out clean. Cool cakes completely before frosting with **Cream Cheese Tofu Icing** (recipe follows).

Makes 1 9-inch round layer cake, 2 single-layer cakes or 1 9 x 13" cake, 16 servings

PER SERVING OF PLAIN CAKE: 282 calories, 5 g protein, 35 g carbohydrate, 14 g total fat (1 g saturated fat, 7 g mono, 5 g poly fat), 40 mg cholesterol, 1 g dietary fiber, 600 RE vitamin A, 12 mcg folate, 2 mg vitamin C, 231 mg sodium, 209 mg potassium, 2 mg iron, 81 mg calcium

# Cream Cheese Tofu Icing

| | |
|---:|:---|
| 8 oz. | cream cheese, at room temperature |
| ½ cup | butter, at room temperature |
| 1 cup | puréed medium *or* firm tofu |
| 1 cup | icing (confectioner's) sugar |
| 1 tsp. | vanilla extract |
| 1½ tsp. | lemon juice |
| ½ | lemon, zest of |

Cream together cream cheese, butter, puréed tofu, and sugar. Fold in remaining ingredients. Any leftover icing or frosted cake can be frozen for up to 2 months.

PER 1 TBSP. SERVING: 68 calories, 2 g protein, 4 g carbohydrate, 5 g total fat (3 g saturated fat, 1 g mono, 1 g poly fat), 14 mg cholesterol, trace dietary fiber, 52 RE vitamin A, 3 mcg folate, trace vitamin C, 46 mg sodium, 25 mg potassium, 1 mg iron, 20 mg calcium

# Lemon Loaf

THIS TANGY, LEMON–FLAVORED cake is a teatime favorite. I like to keep a loaf in the freezer for unexpected guests.

| | |
|---|---|
| I cup | sugar |
| ¼ cup | butter, softened |
| 2 | eggs, separated |
| ½ cup | soft tofu |
| ½ | lemon, juice of |
| I½ cups | unbleached flour |
| I tsp. | baking powder |
| I | lemon, zest of |

### Lemon Glaze

| | |
|---|---|
| ½ cup | sugar |
| I | lemon, juice of |

Cream butter and sugar together in a small bowl.

Beat egg whites until soft peaks form

In a medium bowl with an electric hand blender, blend together egg yolks, tofu, and lemon juice. Fold in sugar and butter mixture, flour, baking powder, lemon zest, and beaten egg whites. Spread batter evenly in a lightly greased loaf pan. Bake at 350°F for about 50 minutes, or until toothpick inserted in center comes out clean. Let cool 5 minutes.

Combine glaze ingredients.

With a toothpick, poke 10 to 15 holes in top of cake. Spoon glaze over it. Cool cake completely before removing it from pan.

Makes 1, 3 x 4 x 8" loaf, 8 to 10 servings

PER SERVING: 253 calories, 4 g protein, 46 g carbohydrate, 6 g total fat (3 g saturated fat, 2 g mono, trace poly fat), 55 g cholesterol, trace dietary fiber, 65 RE vitamin A, 6 mcg folate, 6 mg vitamin C, 99 mg sodium, 48 mg potassium, I mg iron, 44 mg calcium

# Chocolate Brownies

THESE MOIST AND fudgy brownies contain half the butter and half the eggs of the original recipe. If you like chocolate, you'll love these!

| | |
|---|---|
| 1½ cups | sugar |
| ½ cup | butter, at room temperature |
| ½ cup | soft tofu |
| ½ cup | buttermilk |
| 2 | eggs |
| 1 tsp. | vanilla extract |
| 1 cup | unbleached flour |
| ¾ cup | unsweetened cocoa |
| ¾ tsp. | baking powder |
| ½ tsp. | salt |
| ¾ cup | chopped pecans |

### Chocolate Frosting

| | |
|---|---|
| 1 cup | icing (confectioner's) sugar |
| ¼ cup | unsweetened cocoa |
| 2 tbsp. | butter, at room temperature |
| 2 tbsp. | mashed soft tofu |

**Preheat oven to 350°F.**

With electric mixer, beat sugar, butter, and tofu until smooth. Beat in buttermilk, eggs and vanilla. Gradually mix in flour, cocoa, baking powder, and salt. When smooth, fold in pecans.

Spread batter evenly in a lightly greased 9 x 13" baking dish. Bake about 30 minutes or until a toothpick inserted in center comes out clean. Let cool in pan on wire rack.

Cream all frosting ingredients together in a small bowl.

Spread frosting over brownies with a spatula while brownies are still a bit warm. Cool completely; cut into squares.

Makes 24 brownies

PER FROSTED BROWNIE: 170 calories, 2 g protein, 24 g carbohydrate, 8 g total fat (3 g saturated fat, 3 g mono, 1 g poly fat), 31 mg cholesterol, .4 g dietary fiber, 67 RE vitamin A, 6 mcg folate, 1 mg vitamin C, 124 mg sodium, 52 mg potassium, .4 mg iron, 30 mg calcium

# Bunes

THESE CRISP, DEEP-FRIED dough pastries are a specialty of the Dauphiné region of France where they are eaten to celebrate Mardi Gras.

| | |
|---:|:---|
| ½ cup | soft tofu |
| 2 | eggs |
| ¼ cup | dark rum *or* brandy |
| 2 cups | unbleached flour |
| 2 tsp. | baking powder |
| ¼ tsp. | (scant) salt |
| ⅓ cup | butter, at room temperature |
| | oil for frying |
| | granulated sugar to sprinkle on bunes |

In a small bowl, with a hand blender, blend together tofu, eggs, and rum until smooth. Set aside.

In a medium bowl, mix together flour, baking powder, and salt. Cut in butter with a pastry blender until mixture is evenly crumbly. Add liquids and knead into a soft elastic dough. Shape into a 6" log and cover. Let rest about 30 minutes.

Cut log into 3 or 4 pieces. Generously coat a large wooden board with flour. Roll out the first piece of dough very thin. Turn over; roll out again; sprinkle dough and board with flour, if sticky. With a zigzag pastry cutter, cut dough into different shapes (rectangles, squares or triangles—be creative!) each measuring about 4 x 4". Cut one to two 2-inch slits into the center of each bune. Repeat with rest of dough.

In a wok or deep frying pan heat enough oil to cover the bunes (about 3" deep). Heat oil to 365°F or until bubbles start to form. Fry the bunes in batches of 3 to 5 for 2 to 3 minutes, turning them for even browning. Bunes are cooked through when just light golden in color.

Remove bunes from oil with a slotted spoon. Drain on paper towels. Generously sprinkle bunes with sugar; transfer bunes to a serving platter; pile into a little pyramid for a stunning presentation.

Makes 20 to 24, 4-inch square bunes

PER BUNE: 77 calories, 2 g protein, 8 g carbohydrate, 3 g total fat (2 g saturated fat, 1 g mono, trace poly fat), 25 mg cholesterol, 0 g dietary fiber, 33 RE vitamin A, 2 mcg folate, 0 mg vitamin C, 87 mg sodium, 17 mg potassium, .4 mg iron, 32 mg calcium

# Cream Puff Fritters

THESE DELICATE LITTLE pastries are addictive, so allowing only 5 per person can be regarded as stingy by some! Serve them on their own or with sliced fresh fruit. For a sinfully good dessert, serve them with the **Brandy-Soaked Oranges with Almond Lemon Cream** (p. 153).

| | |
|---|---|
| ¾ cup | milk |
| ½ cup | soft tofu |
| 2 tbsp. | butter |
| 3 tsp. | sugar |
| I tsp. | vanilla |
| I cup | unbleached flour |
| 3 | eggs |
| | oil for deep-frying |
| | sugar to sprinkle on fritters |

In a medium saucepan, with a hand blender, blend together milk and tofu until smooth. Add butter, sugar and vanilla; stir while heating. As soon as mixture boils, add the flour, combining quickly with a wooden spoon until mixture forms a smooth ball and detaches itself from the pan. Reduce heat to low; continue stirring another minute, making sure all the flour granules have disappeared and the ball is of a uniform consistency. Remove from heat.

Add the eggs, 1 at a time, using an electric mixer. The dough will at first be broken up into pieces but after further blending it will become smooth. Cover and refrigerate until ready to use. Dough can be made a day ahead to this point.

In a wok or deep frying pan, heat enough oil to cover fritters (about 2" deep). Heat oil to 365°F or until bubbles start to form. Make the fritters in 2 batches. Scoop up a heaping teaspoon of dough and, with another teaspoon, scrape it into the hot oil. Work close to the oil to prevent splattering.

Fry fritters 5 to 7 minutes, turning them for even browning. Remove fritters with a slotted spoon and drain on paper towels. Transfer to a serving dish and generously sprinkle them with sugar. Serve as soon as possible.

Makes about 30, or 6 to 8 servings

PER FRITTER: **37** calories, I g protein, 4 g carbohydrate, 2 g total fat (I g saturated fat, trace mono, trace poly fat), 24 mg cholesterol, 0 dietary fiber, 21 RE vitamin A, 3 mcg folate, trace vitamin C, 18 mg sodium, 20 mg potassium, .2 mg iron, 11 mg calcium

# Eggless Chocolate Cake

THIS LOW-FAT, lightly sweetened cake takes just a few minutes to put together. I got the recipe from my daughter Lara who whips it up whenever one of her friends has a birthday.

| | |
|---|---|
| 1½ cups | unbleached flour |
| 1 cup | sugar |
| 1 tsp. | *each,* baking powder, baking soda |
| 3 tbsp. | unsweetened cocoa |
| ½ cup | soft *or* medium tofu |
| ½ cup | warm water |
| 1 tsp. | white vinegar |
| 1 tsp. | vanilla extract |
| 3 tbsp. | vegetable oil |

In a medium bowl, combine dry ingredients. In a small bowl, with an electric hand blender, blend together tofu, water, vinegar, vanilla, and oil. Mix into dry ingredients until smooth. Pour into lightly greased cake pan. Bake at 350°F for 35 to 40 minutes, or until a toothpick inserted in the center comes out clean. Serve plain or with **Chocolate Frosting** (p. 180).

Makes 1, 8-inch square cake, 16 servings

PER SERVING OF PLAIN CAKE: 121 calories, 2 g protein, 22 g carbohydrate, 3 g total fat (trace saturated fat, 1 g mono, 1 g poly fat), trace cholesterol, trace dietary fiber, 4 RE vitamin A, trace folate, trace vitamin C, 104 mg sodium, 18 mg potassium, 1 mg iron, 28 mg calcium

# INDEX

## H

Hearty Biscuits, 22–23
Herbed Bread Pancakes, 105
Holiday Cranberry/Apricot Soda
    Bread, 28–29
Honey Garlic Peanut Sauce, 65
Honey Twist, 32–33
hot pepper sauce, 49, 52, 55, 88
Hot Wonton Crisps, 52

## I

Italian Bruschetta, 53

## L

Leek and Potato Soup, 72
leeks, 72–73
Lemon Loaf, 179
Lemon Squares, 168–169
lentils, 114
Lime and Ginger Mussels, 49
Low-Fat Chicken/Turkey Burgers,
    140

## M

Macaroni and Cheese, 118
Mango Couscous, 100
mangos, 100

maple syrup, 13–14, 93
Mashed Parsnips, 93
Meat Sauce, 144
Meatballs with Tomato Sauce, 141
Mediterranean Pizza, 34–35
Miniature Dumpling Soup, 71
Mixed Bean Chili, 145
Multigrain Health Bread, 30–31
Mushroom and Tofu Medley, 91
mushrooms, 34, 91, 109, 119, 123,
    136, 142, 144, 146, 148
mussels, 49

## N

No-Bake Lemon Cheesecake Pie,
    155
nuts, pine, 81

## O

oat bran, 134
olives, 34, 81
olives, Kalamata, 38
Onion Bacon Quiche, 37
onions, 34, 37–38, 40, 42–45, 58,
    73–74, 77, 81, 88, 90–91, 100,
    105, 111–114, 119, 123,
    126–129, 132, 138, 140–146,
    148
onions, green, 49–51, 92, 102, 110
onions, red, 77
onions, sweet, 61
orange juice, 65, 164, 170, 172

# W

walnuts, 26, 30, 176
wheat bran, 18, 134
wheat germ, 24, 98, 101, 128,
    141, 166, 168, 172
wheathearts, 103
white wine, dry, 74, 116, 122, 132,
    148
Winter Vegetable Soup, 73
wontons, 50–52

# Y

yogurt, plain, 37, 68, 126, 134,
    164, 172

# Z

Zesty Zucchini, 88
zucchini, 88, 110, 142